Foreword

By John Hutchinson, President & founder of the Amersham & District Motor Bus Society

John welcomes you on board for this trip down memory lane

I can't tell you how pleased I am that Neil Lamond has agreed to write a follow up edition of "The Pride of Bucks". I started driving buses out from the old Amersham garage back in 1971, from the outset I felt the history and camaraderie at the garage should be recognised in a book. For forty years I gathered material. In the mid-1980s it was even announced in The Bucks Free Press that I was writing the book. However, it never materialised and certainly wouldn't have done without the large amount of additional research and writing skills offered by Neil. This book now provides a wonderfully comprehensive account of the vehicles, staff and impact the operation had on the community. Tracing the highs and lows, from being one of the most vital public services in wartime to its decline as private car ownership became almost universal. This story shows how many of the staff extended their work beyond the services for which they were paid, taking a pride in their role within the local community. It will take all readers down a memory lane filled with pleasure.

Front cover from a 1932 Green Line poster, image copyright TfL from the London Transport Museum collection. Rear cover painting by Malcolm Drabwell; he painted this 1942 wartime scene for the 50th anniversary celebrations of Amersham Garage held in 1985. Whilst the garage remained in use, a framed print presented by Malcolm was displayed in the canteen. Photograph above taken by John Golding of a young John Hutchinson at work.

First Published in 2018 by Hawkes Design & Publishing Ltd. – www.hawkesdesign.co.uk

1

Chapters

ACKNOWLEDGEMENTS

Staff at the London Transport Museum, the British Library, Bucks Examiner, Mike Dewey at Bucks Free Press, the Buckinghamshire Centre for Studies, the Coroner's Office, Beaconsfield; Peter Chapman, Peter Wilks, Alan Cross, David Packer, Richard Proctor, Paul Dodge, Paul Lacey, Philip Kirk (Bus Archive), Philip and Wendy Higgs, Norman Freeman, Ian Read, Brian Jones (LBM), Michael Baker (LBM), Allan Oxley (OS), Ron Bovingdon, Maurice Gettings, Wally Lally, Frank Brown, Barry Wilkinson, Kevin Hull, Graham Palser, Michael Rooum, Clive Birch.

THIS BOOK IS DEDICATED TO HENRY, HUGO AND ARABELLA

Introduction

Following the welcome success of "The Pride of Bucks," the history of the Amersham and District Motor Bus Co. 1919–1933. I am pleased you are reading "The Pride of Bucks - Next Destination". This work traces the history of the London Transport operation that built Amersham's art-deco bus garage in 1935 and follows the subsequent operators until its demolition in 1992. The site then becoming part of the Tesco's supermarket we see today.

Through this journey we will step out of black and white and into a world of colour. We study the operating company, its staff, vehicles and routes and their impact on the local community. For those who have read the previous book I apologise for repeating a small number of the photographs and references, this has been done only to allow each book to stand alone as a fuller historical account of the events during each of the eras covered. The photographs used should provide the reader with an image of almost every vehicle type operated from Amersham throughout the period.

We must be thankful for the foresight shown by Edward Curling Miles (born: 13th July 1878; died 17th June 1921) as at the end of The Great War he recognised the need to run motor bus services in and out of Amersham and Chesham. Edward and a syndicate of investors, including his father and other relatives, got together and started the first service in May 1919 running a 26-seat single deck Scout omnibus out to High Wycombe.

Edward Curling Miles driving this lovely car, in a photograph possibly taken around the time of the founding of Amersham & District Motor Bus and Haulage Company.
Photograph courtesy of the Miles family.

Edward had a background in motor vehicles and is recorded in London as a mechanical engineer and motor vehicle driver (domestic) as early as 1903. By 1918 he had established his motor business at Ye Olde Griffin Garage, Amersham, operating behind The Griffin Hotel on The Broadway. The omnibus and haulage business would trade as The Amersham and District Motor Bus & Haulage Company for four months before it launched as a limited liability entity on 15th September 1919. Shares in this enterprise were then freely available to the public for £1/-/- each. In the prospectus the company boasts gross trading figures of £764/12/3 for their first 3 months and 5 days of operation. The directors claimed the business was a "progressive one and capable of considerable extension and they feel confident it will shew (sic) first-class results with the addition of extra vehicles." Their belief eventually proved to be well founded as The Amersham and District Motor Bus Co. handed over 48 vehicles (buses and coaches) to the newly formed London Passenger Transport Board on 24th November 1933. In this book we will see that at its peak the new Amersham Bus Garage would go on to employ about 200 staff; engaged as drivers, conductors, inspectors, maintenance engineers, cashiers, clerical staff, caterers and cleaners; thus, making it a major employer in the town. The canteen not only catered for the staff working from the depot but also visiting crews from other garages and most especially the Green Line drivers and conductors a long way from home at the end of the first leg of their journey. At its height, around forty Green Line vehicles would visit daily from Crawley, Swanley and Godstone garages.

With the brand-new Amersham garage being completed in 1935 an entirely new "modern face" was given to the hub of the business. An up-to-date vision that at the time wasn't entirely extended to the vehicles they operated. However, running old vehicles along the Chiltern's grass-bordered roads possibly smoothed the symmetry of man-made highways and allowed the vehicles to blend in and harmonise with the untouched countryside. In our journey through these pages we encounter dramatic change, from the horrors of a world war to a golden era where the bus symbolised freedom. We encounter friction between management and staff who felt let down and degraded and then we finally bear witness to the decline of a once proud institution. However, we will see how the staff remained a force for good within the community, a number still playing that role today through their efforts in running the Amersham & District Motor Bus Society.

Some of the paragraphs written in italics are created as being the contemporary thoughts of employees at the time. When reading these, please be assured that all the facts are as stated, but some of the circumstances have been created by the author in order to "set the scene" for a better reader experience. I am deeply sad to report that Pete Chapman, son of Jim who appears in many such paragraphs, passed away only a few weeks before this book went to print. I thank him greatly for the inspiration he gave me in penning some of this text.

ADDITIONAL INFORMATION ABOUT A&D MOTOR BUS Co.

Since writing "The Pride of Bucks," a little bit of new information has come to light. In the original Appendix I on page 87, the existence of two Guy double-deckers that A&D had bought second-hand in January 1931 is recorded. Thanks to Paul Lacey those vehicles can further be reported as:-
Registered YU7375 & YX1833 (given A&D bonnet nos. 1 and 7 respectively), they were both Dodson H6ROS-bodied Guy FCX-type six-wheeler double-deckers.

PLEASE NOTE

For the benefit of those born without experiencing pre-decimal currency figures of pounds, shillings and pence, I offer some simple guidelines.
The pound has remained the same, albeit worth a fraction today of what it was at the outset of this book. The pre-decimal pound was divided into 20 shillings, thus making a shilling worth 5p in today's money; therefore a 10-shilling note would equal our 50p coin. Each shilling was worth 12(d) pennies. Pennies themselves were sub-divided into halves and quarters (known as halfpennies and farthings). Prices were generally written as follows:- £20/12/6 means 20 pounds 12 shillings and six pence. With no pennies in the price it would be written as £20/12/-. If you saw just 1/6 for a price that meant one shilling and sixpence.

Chapter 1   The GENERAL Marches In (1933 – 1934)

Jim Chapman woke early on the morning of Friday 24th November 1933, his mind immediately turned to work. He had been a bus driver with the Amersham & District Motor Bus Co. for eight years and today ownership of the company was transferring to the newly formed London Passenger Transport Board, better known to Jim as London General Omnibus Company. He had a new employer. What would things be like under new bosses? He always felt comfortable working under A&D's Will Randall who had taken him on back in 1925. Where would Will fit into the new operation, where did Jim fit into that new picture?

Jim and his wife Vi, had moved to their brand-new house on Amersham's, The Ridgeway the previous year. He dressed in the dark; he was used to that when on early winter shifts. He had been issued with a new green uniform; this was certainly smarter and far more modern looking than his old A&D long style coat with monogrammed lapels. It had suddenly turned cold this morning and it seemed worse weather was on the way. The insides of the small bedroom windows were a jigsaw of frost, a kaleidoscope of frozen tentacles that diffused the light from the street-lamp.

His walk to work was easy; it only took around ten minutes. It was cold though and his breath was condensing; he felt he was working up a bit of steam, like the engines on the Metropolitan line, but steam that provided no comforting warmth. There were no eggs and bacon he could fry on a shovel and his bus would be equally cold even when it emerged from the shed. November had been exceptionally dry so far, there was no ice on the road; this frost was in the air. As he turned right from the foot of Stanley Hill, he thought of the large number of houses that had been built here in the last 18 months, pondering on the expansion of "MetroLand" as they were calling it. Until now he had been able to take his bus up to Coleshill and look down into the valley of Amersham. A little ribbon of a town, unmolested in centuries, full of cottages out from which ancient folk had gazed – long before the coming of the motor bus. Dwellings placed along the road, short on mathematical straight lines, just schemed and simply devised, no damp courses nor insulation, boasting tiny windows and low ceilings, all of which would incense today's authorities and wiseacres at the Planning Office. If built now they would be condemned and knocked down as being against regulations. But the community rightfully treasured them, then and now. The town sat surrounded, deep in this well of a green amphitheatre, now the fingers of development were spreading away from it, like rising ivy up a wall.

Line of charabancs in High Wycombe c.1926. Fourth in line is probably A&D No. 2.
Original photograph from the Randall Family collection, photographer believed to be Frank Adams of H.W.

Jim thought back to when he had started on the buses, driving the solid-tyred charabancs and the little Oldsmobiles. He recalled Will Randall's story from May 1923 when he had been driving a charabanc. About 11:00 pm one evening running the charabanc as a bus service between Chesham and Amersham, Will had collected an inebriated gentleman by the name of William Gale. Mr Gale was already known to the police, he was a pedlar by trade and a drinker by nature. He became aggressive towards Will and knocked him out with one punch. Will had him taken before the court; Jim was grateful never to have encountered such violence. By now charabancs were dinosaurs from the past; was it only seven years since he lined up in High Wycombe with so many of A&D's competitors all visiting the May festival? Back in 1925 the Company's first reliable bus (a venerable AEC) was still plying its route between Chesham and Amersham, and twice daily to High Wycombe. The locals called it the "Old Dreadnought" and this name had passed into common use even at the garage. It used to get very crowded inside, Jim remembered it as being almost to suffocation. No uncommon feat was for some individuals to hang off the back, holding on by the "eyebrows" was a contemporary term they used.

He was nearly at work and could see the new Brazils sausage factory pouring smoke into the pre-dawn sky. He remembered a London General poster from 1924; it showed the unmolested Amersham that had risen in his memory, just then Mr Welch the butcher from Whieldon Street passed him, driving his little van, he tooted, Jim gave an acknowledging wave, he still knew everyone and they knew him.

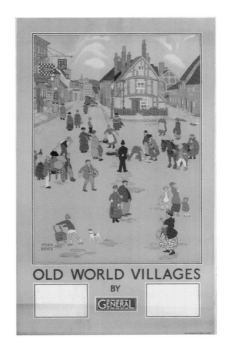

1924 LONDON GENERAL OMNIBUS poster by Helen Bryce
Reproduced courtesy of the London Transport Museum

The Helen Bryce poster comes to life as Jim remembers GENERAL charabancs rumbling into Amersham a decade earlier. Talk about "tanks on A&D's front lawn," these coaches had parked directly opposite the front of The Griffin Pub, the founding home of Jim's beloved A&D.
Photograph by kind permission of Bill Perren family.

Conspiracy theories fermented in his brain, back in 1924 London General were promoting their pleasant charabanc trips to visit "Old World Villages" and now just 9 years on, the "GENERAL" were moving in. They were moving in today, they were part of the change this time. We were being told it was because the Government wanted greater streamlined transport integration, but was this empire building by the stiff white collars at Head Office?

For many weeks, different "GENERAL" livered vehicles had been turning up on the garage forecourt. In fact, the first vehicle he had seen sporting the General's green and black colours was actually a new Gilford AS6 20-seater that had been bought by A&D in the summer.
This new ownership had been a long time in the planning and today was the day. The staff were not told where these other vehicles were from, they did know the plan was to rationalise vehicle types at different locations across the new network. Though there seemed little pattern to Jim, everything that has turned up so far was different. Jim and his colleagues were interested in how they would drive and they quickly got opportunities to take them out on service. Soon the conductors and cleaners were saying "Oh this one's come from Maidstone & District, I found an old ticket tucked away in a crack, and this one's come from ……."

7

Shown above is the very last vehicle purchased by Amersham & District Bus Co. This coach is seen brand new in the summer of 1933 outside Strachan's Acton factory building. Unusually for the Company it was a Gilford, registered ABH366, a model AS6 20-seater, looking very luxurious with curtains at the windows. The coach was given A&D bonnet no. 38. The vehicle appears to be finished in the London General Country Bus green & black colour scheme and lacks either the A&D or GENERAL name. The photograph is taken about six months before A&D were officially taken over by L.P.T.B.

Photo John Hutchinson collection.

Jim's new green overcoat, would stand the test of time, this type was issued unchanged between 1933 and 1963.

Image courtesy of London Transport Museum collection.

None of the buses had any heaters, so it would continue to be a cold day whatever vehicle he was issued. But shortly they would all be throwing up the crisp dry tawny autumn leaves into golden brown vortex clouds as they drove off the forecourt and swept into the Buckinghamshire countryside for their duties that day. Jim hoped little would change his happy driving days in the Chilterns even under new management and, after all, it was Friday; Friday was pay day and that always put a smile on his face.

A&D handed over to the London Passenger Transport Board (LPTB) 48 vehicles on 24th November 1933. The fleet was made up as follows:-

5 x Dennis 2.5 ton
1 x Dennis 3.4 ton
10 x Dennis E
1 x Dennis EV
1 x Dennis 30cwt
1 x Dennis F
4 x Dennis G & GL
1 x Dennis Lancet
4 x Gilford (30/32 seaters)
3 x Gilford AS6
2 x AEC Regent lowbridge double-deckers
11 x AEC Regal "T" Class
3 x Chevrolets
1 x AJS Pilot

This was already a very mixed bag of vehicles that the new owners would wish to rationalise in the shortest period of time. The thirteen AECs were their only real blessing and already matched the forward planning for LPTB. The Chevrolets, AJS and some of the Gilfords went in a short space of time, whilst a few of the other Gilfords were moved to different garages. Surprisingly the very early Dennis 2.5 ton vehicles soldiered on at Amersham and can be seen in a number of photographs. It must be remembered at this stage that the 48 vehicles had come from the two A&D garages (Amersham and High Wycombe) and as this book is only about Amersham we will now go on to study those vehicles that remained in operation there. However, for at least five years Amersham seemed to miss out on the true benefits of rationalising its fleet. Instead of decreasing the number of variant makes in use at the garage, LTPB actually increased it by adding manufacturer models from Morris, Bedford, Daimler, Thorneycroft, Tilling-Stevens and Saurer. This put untold pressure on the engineering staff trying to keep this huge variety of makes in serviceable condition.

For a while the old A&D route structure was run unchanged. At the same time as LPTB were rebranding the buses with the "General" image the garage put out a 1d timetable booklet dated "November 1933". This was in fact an Amersham & District one that hastily had "LONDON TRANSPORT (Amersham & District Motor Bus & Haulage Co. Ltd.)" placed on the front cover, whilst inside everything remained A&D typeset text even down to the "Passenger Regulations" which were credited as being from A&D. An advertisement within, offered buses and coaches from 14 to 32 seats on hire from A&D. In fact, we know from the old A&D account books that they still invoiced private hire vehicles under the A&D name for up to a year after the takeover.

From a viewpoint behind the arches underneath the old Market Hall building, a nicely framed photograph has been created of the former A&D Dennis 2.5 ton, bonnet number 6, PP7144 as it runs into Old Amersham passed The Kings Arms.
Photograph courtesy of the A B Cross collection.

Green Line Coaches had started operations in July 1930, their luxury AEC Regal T-type vehicles setting new standards for the travelling passenger. The coaches sported a new sage green and black livery and the hand-picked staff chosen to operate them had the importance of "Service, comfort and speed with safety" impressed on them by the Head Office management at Reigate. By October 1931 Green Line had 275 coaches operating on 27 different routes across the wider Home Counties network. Although the routes that ran from Amersham were initially done under the Amersham and District Motor Bus Company banner, they were by all intents and purposes, standard Green Line services and vehicles. So pleased were LGOC with the Green Line concept that they registered the names Blue Line, Red Line and Yellow Line to thwart imitators.

On 17th January 1934 Green Line who took over all coach routes in our area and extended its route "B" (Wrotham-Rickmansworth) to Chesham and Aylesbury, offering a two-hourly service. This eliminated the need to shuttle Chesham people to Amersham to pick up the coach service.

Over the coming pages, photographs illustrate the evolution of bus branding as LPTB undertake livery changes to its newly inherited local fleet.

GT1657 Dennis Arrow dating from 1931. The Arrow was the predecessor to the Lancet (shown in the photograph below which itself was a model that A&D bought to run alongside its AEC Regals). This photograph shows the 32-seater coach in Green Line livery and sporting bonnet number D5. It seems to be operating on a normal bus service to Ley Hill and the lack of route number possibly places the photograph date to 1934. There can be no absolute certainty this Dennis Arrow is operating from Amersham garage but it seems more than likely. This vehicle would later be re-designated as DL39 and was finally withdrawn from LPTB service in November 1937.
Photograph taken by J F Higham courtesy A B Cross.

This 1932 built Dennis Lancet KX8570 (ex A&D bonnet number 2) shows the next phase of bus branding following the A&D takeover. Here it can be seen in LPTB country bus colours of green and black and with the "GENERAL" brand name. This vehicle was later given the LT bonnet number DT3. It was transferred to Hemel Hempstead and finally sold off in November 1937.
Photograph taken by J F Higham courtesy of A B Cross.

Again we see a former A&D vehicle that has been repainted but retaining its original bonnet number. The 1926 Dennis 2.5 ton PP5454 still displaying its old number 12.
Photograph from the J F Higham collection (courtesy of The Omnibus Society).

On 31ˢᵗ January 1934 ex-A&D routes 21 & 22 to Berkhamsted and Pond Park were withdrawn. Route 21 virtually duplicated the National N6 route taken over already by LPTB. Most residents of Pond Park Estate walked down a footpath to the Berkhampsted Road to catch a bus into Chesham and gain a slightly cheaper fare.

As we can see from contemporary photographs, displaying route numbers on the inherited vehicle fleet was a problem. A&D had never displayed route numbers in their 14 years of operation. Their timetable booklets only started to append a route number in their indexes from August 1931. Their maps only showed the number from February 1932 (see below) but no route numbers were shown on vehicles at this time.

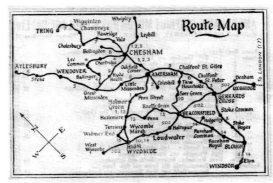

Image courtesy of Paul Dodge collection.

This lovely nearside photograph shows former A&D bonnet no. 21 although the number has been painted out in its new makeover to General colours. Manufactured in 1929 this Dennis E KX2973 shows High Wycombe on the destination blind.
Photograph taken by J F Higham courtesy of A B Cross.

This 1934 photograph now shows a transitional route numbering stage for the new company. A&D only adopted route numbers in the closing months of their existence but they never displayed them on vehicles, merely using them in their timetable booklets. In this photograph taken in Old Amersham the 18-seater Dennis G KP7159 shows it is running on Route 23 to Beaconsfield, so the old A&D route number is now in use by an LPTB bus. From Wednesday 3rd October 1934 all routes out of Amersham were given 300 series numbers and this became the 396.
Photograph from Peter Wilks collection, courtesy of A B Cross.

The LTPB were extremely diligent in appraising all the vehicles inherited by the multitude of takeovers that contributed to the new greater London network. A plan was exacted whereby vehicles were redistributed around the garages to concentrate disparate makes in as few centres as possible, thereby decreasing maintenance costs. The futures of each garage were also assessed and plans put in place to enlarge, build new or close those associated with the recent takeovers. As we will see, Amersham was earmarked for a completely new building along the lines of the one A&D itself had created in High Wycombe, although it must be said that was done in conjunction with London General Omnibus Company at the time.

This is a wonderful photograph showing further transition in 1934. At the back we see KX7634 (A&D bonnet no. 35 that would become T362) still in its A&D livery and centred in the photo is General liveried 1928 AEC designed and so called "Associated Daimler" type 426 registration PH8881. In October 1934 LPTB introduced the new style 300 series route numbers to run out of Amersham and the North Western region. This Daimler was sold out of stock on 27th January 1936.
Photograph taken in Chesham by J F Higham, courtesy of A B Cross.

There were inevitably differentials in pay rates of the staff that moved to LPTB from each of the independents. By the time of the A&D takeover, agreement had been reached with the Transport and General Workers Union (TGWU) on the following pay scales for a 48-hour, 6-day week:-

Green Line drivers	£4/-/-
Country bus drivers	£3/12/6
All conductors	£3/-/-

One-man bus drivers were now given a weekly bonus of 5/- on top of their standard pay rate. We know from A&D records that Jim Chapman was paid £3/5/- per week as a one-man-operator driver from 1926, so presumably his rate would already have exceeded the £3/17/6 that the Board were now offering. Jim also like doing overtime and as Sunday working, bank holidays and overtime attracted enhanced remuneration he probably fared rather well.

Right up until the end of the 1930s there were far fewer actual bus stops in the country area, passengers were free to hail the bus pretty much when and where they liked. However, the LPTB embarked on a visionary plan to erect stylish green and black liveried shelters at important traffic points along coach and country bus routes, thereby creating mini bus stations rather akin to "halts" on the railways. A design by Mr Charles Holden of Adams, Holden and Pearson, architects to the Board, was agreed upon. Each up-to-date shelter would offer a

14

measure of comfort and be an information point with route map and timetables displayed. In addition, a special canopy type of shelter was also designed when space was limited. The planned erection of these was a major undertaking and was going to be a long time in full implementation. Where there were still no formal stopping posts, timetables were posted in frames attached to buildings, usually pubs and other community-based facilities.

A picturesque 1934 view of a new Charles Holden designed "London Transport" bus shelter at Chalfont St. Giles as captured in June that year.
Image Copyright TfL from the London Transport Museum collection.

The above photo shows how the A&D garages and the brick-built offices at Amersham would have looked on the day of the takeover. Lined up outside the sheds are a rather disparate looking collection of vehicles, on the left is a large single-deck Gilford, next to it a Tilling Stevens (KM3866) and the GENERAL liveried vehicle with the lady standing in front of it, is a little Chevrolet U.
Photo courtesy Michael Rooum.

This second shot of the garage from around the same time (1934) shows three Green Line vehicles. On the left, T359 KX7886 (ex A&D); at the far end a Green Line coach on Route R, both are sandwiching a smaller 20-seat Saurer 2AD bus XY5337 dating from 1925, this was often used on a shuttle service from Chesham to connect with the London bound coach.

Photograph by the late D W K Jones, courtesy of the A D Packer collection.

A final forecourt picture from this short period shows a 1929 20-seat Gilford CP6 model UP3137. This bus had enjoyed a short period working with Biggerstaff's Bus Services in Sarratt before the LPTB takeover in November 1933. Anyone familiar with Sarratt today will know that Biggerstaffs still run a motor repair and petrol garage in the village.

Photograph from the J F Higham collection, courtesy of A B Cross.

This low-bridge AEC Regent is running on the 336 route. Later it will be issued an ST fleet number but for the moment is solely registered as GF7218.
Photograph taken by J F Higham courtesy of A B Cross.

Accidents will happen....

On 30th June 1934 William Arthur Brown of Pond Park, Chesham was driving his LPTB bus, working out of Amersham Garage on the Slough route. Just after midday and between Gerrards Cross and Stoke Poges he felt a loss of power and virtually ground to a halt, however, he managed to get the vehicle to the side grass verge. Seemingly unable to facilitate a roadside repair, some passengers decided to try and flag down vehicles to get lifts to complete their onward journeys to Slough. One vehicle stopped forward of the bus to pick up a few people, just as he did so, a lorry came around the bend in the opposite direction narrowly missing his car but striking the rear three panels of the bus. Mr Brown and conductor, Mr Stanley Mills of "The Firs" Station Road, Amersham gave evidence against the lorry driver in court. The defendant claimed the bus was sticking out too far, but a bus passenger stated that this claim was totally untrue. The lorry driver was fined £2 for "careless driving" and ordered to pay £1/3/4 in costs, his licence was also endorsed.

The Police take a dim view of Green Line drivers speeding.

It was reported in a Bucks Examiner in June 1934 that Redvers Frank Mayo of "Engledyke" Stanley Hill, Amersham had been recorded driving a coach at between 45 and 48 mph over three quarters of a mile stretch of road between Chalfont St. Giles and Amersham. The police stopped him and he denied the charge but did say his speedometer was not working and he doubted the coach was even capable of such a speed. In court he claimed he was a very safe driver with a "Safety – First" certificate to prove it. He said he did 50,000 miles per annum and 30,000 of that in London traffic. He never knew which vehicle he was to drive on any one day but felt he was a fair judge of speed. Mr Mayo agreed he had lost a bit of time in Shepherds Bush (Route R) earlier but was not trying to make that up when he was stopped. The defendant was fined £3/0/0 but retained his clean licence.

Following on; in the Bucks Examiner in December 1934 - Sidney Francis Griffin of Highland Road, Amersham driving the Wrotham – Aylesbury coach (Route B) was pulled over by police at The Gate public house in Chorley Wood. They had been chasing him on the new road from Chalfont Station to Chenies since they turned left from the top of Stoney Lane. "His speed was well in excess of 50 mph" they told the court. On being pulled over the defendant said "I am late, I should have been in Rickmansworth by now." Public Service Vehicle coaches were restricted by law to 30 mph and Sidney was fined £2/0/0 and had his, otherwise clean, licence endorsed. It would probably be headlined as "A Fare Cop" in today's press; in 1934 it was given the title "A MOTOR COACH DOES "FIFTY"".

In both the above cases the police officers involved were Constables Taylor and Bright.

Two members of the former A&D fleet (numbered 14 & 15 respectively) that were initially given the GENERAL's clothes but rapidly found themselves no longer required. PP7700 is a diminutive 14-seater Dennis 30 cwt from 1927 and KX470 a far grander 30-seater Dennis F all-weather coach from 1928. Both photographed around the time of their disposal by LPTB in 1934/5.
Photographs courtesy A D Packer.

Jim collected his week's wages at the end of his shift on Friday 23rd November 1934 and started his stroll home. He and Vi had just had a son, baby Peter was just two months old and Jim longed to see him after work. Vi had also told him she had a nice bit of liver for his tea, they would make it special tonight, as it was pay day. Walking home that evening he pondered on things at the garage. Gosh, was it one year already since A&D had been taken over? Mr Randall was still there every day, although he had far less to do with the running of a mere single garage now, he was looking after a whole area. Jim thought that things weren't too bad really, his customers were certainly happy and he was still driving his beloved one-man routes. He never really took to crew operations did Jim, and he now got a five-bob weekly bonus for going it alone. But some of the things the Company was doing he couldn't understand; how many different types of vehicles were they going to accumulate at Amersham? And now he has been told they are all being given another new name – "London Transport". Money to burn he thought as he turned to go up Stanley Hill.

From May 1934 the new branding of "London Transport" began to be seen. Uniforms remained the same but a green bulls-eye badge dissected by the words "London Transport" was adopted. In fact, the Board had thought their legal title of London Passenger Transport Board was too long as a brand.

Chapter 2   Routing Out the Future (1935 – 1938)

The title to this chapter could also be called "Rooting out the future" as LT started on the slow task of standardising its massive fleet and getting rid of the more ancient looking carriages. Amersham called for special attention, running around ten different makes of vehicles in addition to models from LPTBs preferred supplier AEC. The number of separate models would have almost doubled that figure. However, planning new routes and integrating what was already under operation would run alongside the vehicle issue.

Having only just applied "GENERAL" logos to the buses running from Amersham it was now all change to re-brand them as "London Transport". We now also start to see the use of stencil garage codes and running numbers appearing on the fleet. Initially the code allocated to Amersham was AM as seen below the driver's window in this next photograph. However, it was soon realised that AM was in use by a Central Area garage at Plumstead and, probably with red faces matching the colour of its central area buses, Amersham's code was hastily changed to MA. However, as it actually meant the stencil could just be inserted in frame in a back to front fashion, no cost would be involved (in practice a small lip would be hammered the other way to facilitate this).

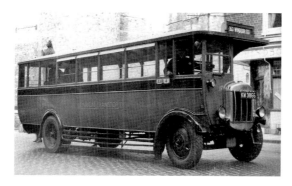

This photo taken at Windsor, probably in early 1935, shows a former Maidstone & District Tilling Stevens (KM3866) operating on Amersham's Route 353 between Chesham and Windsor. The garage code stencil displays the early lettering AM. The number 4 denotes the running number on that route. Also, we now see the new brand logo "London Transport" on the side.
Photograph taken by J F Higham courtesy of A B Cross.

It seems that it wasn't until after February 1935 that the rebranding of the inherited fleet extended to starting the process of giving the vehicles new LT bonnet numbers. The buses and coaches had been sensibly just known by their registration numbers until then. In this interim period either no bonnet number would be seen on the vehicle or in some cases the old A&D number could still be seen. When they were finally issued, some would be seen to be suffixed with either "B" or "C" thus denoting whether they were buses or coaches, these particular suffixes only lasted a few years and were removed at later re-paints.

A Dennis Model G (KP4951) on Route 396 waiting by the old A&D garage sheds to go to Beaconsfield. This bus illustrates the next phase of branding by using the revised garage code stencil MA.
Photograph taken by J F Higham courtesy of A B Cross.

These photographs, taken around 1935, are of Amersham based Harold Foster and Bill Evans (driver and conductor respectively) proudly showing their London Transport uniforms off in front of their Dennis E. Judging from the "OT" registration letters, this vehicle was originally from Aldershot & District's fleet. LT had sold all the Dennis E's operated from Amersham by early 1936 although they were only 6 or 7 years old.
Photograph John Hutchinson collection.

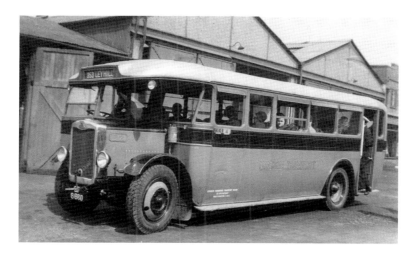

A 32-seat Dennis EV (GF6680) bonnet no. D2 running on Route 353 to Ley Hill but stopping at the old A&D sheds to pick up passengers. This photograph was probably taken in May 1935; the old A&D headquarters building has been re-branded with "London Transport". This vehicle was sold off in April 1936. The EV model had a 6-cylinder engine as opposed to the 4-cylinder fitted to the E models.
Original photograph contains no credit on the reverse, from N Lamond collection.

Dating from May 1935; this photograph of a Dennis 4-ton (PH1106) working Route 359 out to Hyde Heath. The bus and the somewhat puzzled looking driver are waiting outside the cinema on Chesham Broadway. The picture showing that week was Boris Karloff in "House of Doom."
Photograph by the late D W K Jones, courtesy of A D Packer collection.

With the large promotional budget of the Metropolitan Railway constantly selling the virtues of living to the north-west of London it is not surprising that the area started to become popular with ramblers and day tourists. Walks in "Metro-Land" were promoted with the publication of "Country Walk Booklets". So, during the 1930s literally hundreds of people came out to the region every weekend to explore "the gems of the English countryside". Green Line coaches also benefitted well from the exodus out of the "smoke" as did local bus routes serving the prettier villages not on the Met. Line.

KX8644 formerly A&D bonnet no. 4 but now Green Line T366, photographed outside the old A&D headquarters building, branded "GREEN LINE" jointly with "LONDON TRANSPORT".
Photograph courtesy of The Kithead Trust.

At this time, we also slowly start to see a new livery for both Green Line coaches and LT buses. Gone is the black waistband; for Green Line a two-tone green colour scheme and for buses a single green with contrasting roof (generally silver of white).

The old A&D shed style garages had been deemed inadequate for a modern transport system run by LT and plans were drawn up for an entirely new garage to be built on land to the east of the existing site. The building was designed by architects Wallis, Gilbert and Partners who, in 1933, had seen their iconic Hoover Building completed on London's Western Avenue. Construction by J. Jarvis and Sons Ltd. went ahead rapidly.

Another May 1935 photograph, this time of Gilford GF11 operating as a Green Line coach out of Amersham. The new garage is almost ready for occupation and can be seen in the background.
Photograph courtesy of A D Packer

It was Tuesday May 21st 1935 and Jim had been given an early shift as he was one of the privileged invitees to Ye Olde Griffin this evening.

SAFETY FIRST DRIVING AWARDS

On this very special occasion forty-four Safety First Awards were issued to LPTB drivers from Amersham and High Wycombe garages for their safety records the previous year. The presentations were made by C E Ayres, the Operating Superintendent of Country Buses based at Reigate; his Operating Assistant J G Dickins; W Randall, now District Superintendent; District Inspectors G Line and C Mays. Mr Ayres gave an impassioned speech extolling how being extra diligent whilst driving inevitably made for better and safer drivers. Reducing accidents was of paramount importance to the Company.

Will Randall was especially pleased, he was now in a senior position for one of the world's largest bus fleet operators and here he was, sitting back in The Griffin Hotel, Amersham where this local story, in which he had been so instrumental, had begun 16 years earlier. Notwithstanding the fact he was again surrounded by his "lads" who were now doing so well under their new employers. He chuckled at the annotated menu as it caused a lot of good humour, with its appended remarks typed out for each course. "Underslung chassis of pork; Not to be given to Inspectors," "Jellies – Non-skid" and "Biscuits and cheese; Available on day of issue only". Will could not have been happier, things were going well.
(A copy of this menu was printed on page 82 of the previous book, "The Pride of Bucks").

THE AWARDS

Diplomas were awarded to Amersham drivers as follows:-

F Hurst, T Swadling, W J Chapman, F J Brown, W Hance, D Mulkern, S W Francis, L J Harris, W A Brown, R J Merrell, R Simpkins, W Dyer, J Skells, W J Brackley, P C Brazier, F Branham, H A Hall, F G J Rays, R F Mayo, H Rutland, C J W Bowers, R J Williams, A E Halls, S H Reading.

The Penn Bus Company was acquired jointly by the Board and Thames Valley on 1st Aug 1935, their workings went to High Wycombe with the exception of a route from Tylers Green to Beaconsfield which was merged with the 396 out of Amersham.

During the summer of 1935, the new Amersham garage nears completion.
Image courtesy of TfL from the London Transport Museum collection.

The new garage was completed and opened on Wednesday 14th August 1935. The building was 150 ft. x 130 ft. providing a floor area of 19,500 sq. ft. It was estimated to hold up to 54 vehicles, however, the old A&D garages were still retained as extra capacity. Understandably the Board of London Transport's Country Buses and Coaches wasted little time in showing dignitaries around their new flagship premises. Mr A H Hawkins, the Board's General Manager, and Mr E Rawdon Smith, Public relations Officer, certainly took a great deal of pride in the Amersham garage.

Inside the new garage looking to the front. Fuel pumps on the left for the all-important fill-up at the end of each day.
Photograph by kind permission of Bill Perren family.

This photograph was taken in 1935 outside the newly finished garage. It shows an interesting array of vehicles. On the left is a very early AEC Regal, T25 UU6640 which had just arrived at Amersham and stayed until June 1938 when it was withdrawn. Next to it is AEC Reliance, R42B HV66, this stayed at MA until being sold at the beginning of 1939 and finally the one vehicle that allows us to firmly date the photograph is a 20-seater one-man operated Gilford GF127B that was withdrawn in February 1936. Notice in this early photo, and the next one, there are no lights above the outside two garage entrances.
Photograph courtesy of The Omnibus Society.

The new expanded Amersham garage operation had about sixty vehicles based there in 1935. The immense span of the steel cantilever roof was a first for the Board's garages and was shown off with particular aplomb, as it provided a totally unobstructed floor space. Refuelling pumps sited inside were, for safety purposes, fed from tanks placed under the side road outside the building. Fire extinguishers were mounted at intervals around the walls and long skylights filled the arena with daylight. Washing hoses that could be retracted into the roof and "easy clean" pits with white faced bricks were further advanced modern features.

This photograph shows a very smart 31-seat Duple bodied Albion Valkyrie coach AHK984 at Amersham probably in the winter of 1935/6. The destination blinds say (Top) Green Line (Bottom) PRIVATE. Amersham driver Wilf Brackley on the left, not in uniform, engages the driver in conversation. Wilf was already a well-established figure at Amersham Garage having started working as a driver for the old A&D company in February 1931. LT took over 10 Albions (but only one Valkyrie) from various companies; none are recorded as being based at MA. This vehicle was later fitted with a rather incongruous looking destination box of the type seen fitted on EV6168 (see page 28), it was also given bonnet no. AN1c. The vehicle was taken out of LT stock on 11th March 1938. Photograph courtesy of The Omnibus Society.

The offices to the right of the new garage provided a fresh dimension in quality for their staff that now numbered 172 of all grades and types. From the offices it was easy to view the movement of vehicles whilst remaining safe and in a clean, low noise and healthy environment. The building comprised the District Inspector and Depot Engineer's offices, Traffic office, Conductor's room, canteen and boiler room. A further office was provided for none other than W K Randall who, as Superintendent of the Western District, controlled an area about thirty by twenty miles. Glazed hatches, storage rooms and racking were also plentiful, everything combined to give a light and airy feel. The garage would start by serving the eleven bus routes and three coach routes that had been built up around the area. The whole complex was certainly a far cry from the original old army hut, erected back in 1923 to serve as A&D's initial premises following their move from the rear of The Griffin Hotel.

Yet another variant that ran out from the Amersham garage was ex A&D bonnet number 32, an 18-seater Dennis GL model KX5923 dating from October 1930. Shown here running on Route 369A, this vehicle was sold off by London Transport later in 1935.

Photograph courtesy A D Packer.

Looking like the starting grid for a "Wacky Races" cartoon, it aptly illustrates the mismatched selection of buses that Amersham relied upon at this time. The press and dignitaries were given a tour of the new premises in October 1935 and this photo may come from that time. The original is a large format print on card indicating it was a professionally set up image. The ST on the right is ST162 registered GF7218 and the single-decker in front of it is Morris MS5B, PL6462.

Photograph courtesy of Amersham Museum

Standing outside the new garage is 1932 built 30-seat Dennis Lancet EV6168 bonnet no. DT7 painted mid-green with silver roof. This vehicle had been given the destination roof box in a refit in February 1935 and it was immediately transferred to Amersham. It was withdrawn from service in November 1937. We can see the driver reaching up inside the cab to change the destination blind, now set as Route 362B to High Wycombe via Hazelmere and Terriers. The lights above the main garage entrances seem to have been changed already.
Photographed by D W K Jones courtesy A D Packer collection.

In 1935 LT was able to showcase two new main mainstream vehicles. The STL double-decker, of which the new front door 48-seat models were being shown at Hemel Hempstead and the first batch of the extremely modern looking AEC Q-type 38-seat single-deckers. For Amersham the first batch of four Q-types would contribute towards the rationalisation of some from its disparate fleet of mixed models and makes. The "Q" totally departed from previous designs, it was thoroughly modern and could have been launched equally well a decade later. The body design for this vehicle, in departing from the "half-cab" style was an altogether cutting-edge piece of technology, an absolute credit to the planners and draughtsmen at London Transport and AEC. In a contemporary local newspaper report the interior was described as follows "has the entrance at the front (a roomy platform), has a cosy front seat which is by the side of the driver's cabin and is of the nature of an observation box, "easy" seats and plenty of comfort room. The build is on most graceful lines". The Q-types were destined to replace the Dennis Es at Amersham. The two-tone green livery with black waistband and mudguards gave the vehicles an air of class (Author's note: although this colour was on its way out as it was launched). A diesel engine fitted under a long bench seat behind the driver made for a roomier vehicle; however, it could be noisy for passengers. From Amersham they initially started working on the 362 Ley Hill-High Wycombe route in July 1935 and soon afterwards took over some Green Line journeys. Replacements for the smaller Dennis and other odd make buses at Amersham also started to be delivered in 1935. These were in the form of the brand new 20-seat Leyland Cub "C" class vehicles. The Cubs though, did not look that different to the vehicles they were due to replace. They did, however, continue to fulfil the standardisation process that was so sorely needed.

The garage's Sports and Social Club had continued to gain strength since its foundation back in A&Ds' days. The huge children's party held early each year was always a triumph and was provided free of charge by the collection of loose change gathered as the staff came in and out of the canteen. Mr Godbold was at the centre of most organised events of this type. This year there had been a Punch and Judy show and movie apparatus was set up to screen scenes from Bertram Mills' Circus and sketches from Charlie Chaplin and Harold Lloyd. The mums and dads could let their hair down at dance that evening.

On the sporting front; the footballers had won county and bus competitions, with cricket and swimming being highly popular summer month pursuits. Amersham had beaten High Wycombe at tennis that May and their latest venture, the Rifle Club now had thirty members. In total during 1935 the Club numbers were 196 members (148 ordinary and the rest honorary).

GREEN LINE
AT ALL TIMES

Green Line Guide 2ᵈ at all bookstalls

A wonderfully atmospheric Green Line poster from 1936 showing early morning boarding of a T-type coach.
Image copyright TfL from the London Transport Museum collection.

The Route R from Chesham to Oxford Circus (via Amersham, Chalfonts, Uxbridge, Shepherds Bush) ran hourly in 1936 at a cost of 3/3 return or 55/- 4-weekly. Passengers could only board at Green Line stop signs when the coach was between Uxbridge and London. In the country you could still hail the coach or alight anywhere.

In May 1936 London Transport started to experiment with local discounted weekly tickets on some buses. Examples of which would be Chesham to Amersham, ordinary single fare 4d, weekly fare 2/8; Amersham (Crown) to Chalfont St Peter, ordinary single 7d, weekly fare 4/8. They promoted them as being "12 bus rides at the cost of 8". Scholars could save further money by buying fifty tickets.

This photograph shows a one-man-operated Bedford 20-seater BD5B registration AKM 308 passing the windmill at Cholesbury on Route 397 to Tring LT Garage. It was taken in August 1936 and the vehicle was only used at Amersham for a few months that year. It was withdrawn from LT service in July 1938.
Image courtesy of TfL from the London Transport Museum collection.

LPTB Crossing Swords with Mr Dell's Rover Bus Service

LPTB were fearfully protective about their status as the only local licence holder to carry fare paying passengers on "stage carriage" journeys. In June 1936 Mr Jesse Dell was taken to court when he was accused of running a "stage carriage" service serving two separate dances that had taken place six months earlier. Earnest Paveley an inspector with the Board was a witness, he stated that tickets were sold to take customers back to Chesham from the Amersham dances. Mr Dell successfully claimed it was the dance hall organisers who had asked for money as they had hired him privately and any payment he received came from the dance organisers and not the passengers. The Judge dismissed the case.

The 1935/6 safe driver awards were held in June at High Wycombe. The successful drivers from Amersham were C J Bowers, W Brackley, F Branham, W A Brown, E Coleman, A Easton, E Easton, H A Halls, W Hance, R J Merrell, D Mulkern, H Purves, F Rayes, S Reading, C Sharp, G Stokes, B W Wallis, G W Walsh, R J Williams and H J Wright.

Some local rural country lanes were now under threat; Metroland was expanding. In August 1936 a front page article in the Bucks Examiner was titled:-

"IMPROVEMENTS" IN CHARTRIDGE LANE

A photograph on the cover page showed workman stripping back trees as road widening measures were undertaken. The caption beneath read ""Modernisation" of Chartridge Lane – a sign of progress but many regret that the winding old lane is to lose its identity and rurality". Once again, we see resistance to change, a regret that the old ways were being swept aside in the drive to criss-cross the Chilterns in tarmac.

From October 1936 four new T-type coaches (T413, T422, T433, T439) were put into use at the garage. The promotional material released to the press in June said they were "very neat 30-seat coaches with tubular seats upholstered in porous rubber and with an ingenious system of heating and ventilation. A conveniently placed handle allowing all windows to be adjusted to any desired height". Known officially as 9T9s these front entrance coaches allowed the replacement of further "inherited" vehicles such as any remaining Gilfords. But it wasn't long before their smaller 7.7 litre diesel engines were found to be under-powered for long haul work and they only stayed at Amersham until June 1938.

A particularly interesting 1936 scene on Chesham Broadway. The cinema is showing "Broadway Melody 1936" and "Night Mail". Cars and bicycles are freely parked at the road's edge and the 316 arriving from Bovingdon has to double park. The bus is a 3-year old Morris Viceroy YB6 20-seater with fleet number MS1B (registered AKJ872).
Photograph from the J F Higham collection, courtesy of A B Cross.

A very shiny and newly refurbished 1930 built T378B, this photograph was taken around 1936 in Uxbridge. The vehicle is operating on the unusually numbered Route 455 and has the garage code MA clearly visible, the 455 was generally operated by High Wycombe garage vehicles. This route was formerly run by A&D. The bus was taken out of London Country service in 1939.
Photograph courtesy of The Omnibus Society

On Thursday 10th December 1936 King Edward VIII abdicated and the following evening, he made a worldwide radio broadcast from Windsor Castle and famously said "I found it impossible to carry the heavy burden of responsibility and to discharge my duties as king as I would wish to do without the support of the woman I love". Wilf Brackley was working a late shift that day on the 353 and when he got home that night his wife told him the King had been on the radio from Windsor; Wilf and his passengers had been feet away from history!

Heavy snow in The Chilterns causes chaos

As February 1937 came to a close, a blizzard struck The Chilterns leaving up to 7-foot snow drifts in its wake. Several buses didn't make it back to the garage the night it struck.

This shadowy old photo taken on Monday 1st March shows Morris YB6 HA7041 (also seen in the next photo) stuck in a drift whilst on Route 394 at South Heath. Locals are trying their best to get her out as she had been there all night. That Sunday two more buses had been firmly stranded by the "Barley Mow" at Hyde Heath in 4 to 5 feet drifts, one of them had also sunken into soft ground. Neither returned to the garage that night nor did a double-decker stuck at Holmer Green but a single-decker held in deep snow at Wigginton did make it back that night.

Photograph from The Bucks Examiner courtesy of The British Library.

This 1936 or 37 photograph shows 20-seater Morris YB6 with London Transport
bonnet no. MS2. It had been bought new in 1930 and taken over by LGCS in April
1932. It was repainted this two-tone green colour with silver roof and black
mudguards during 1935. It finished its days working out of Amersham and is seen
here on the 398 route to Beaconsfield (Saracen's Head) via Coleshill. It was
withdrawn in October 1937.

Photograph taken by D W K Jones courtesy of A D Packer collection.

THE DERBY · JUNE 2

SPECIAL COACHES DIRECT TO THE COURSE

From	Depart	Return fare, Children half-fare	Booking Agents
	a.m.		
Chesham	8.45		Mr. R. Wright, Broadway, Chesham (CHESHAM 32)
Amersham (Oakfield Corner)	8.55	7/6	Bucks Insurance Bureau Ltd., Oakfield Corner, Amersham (AMERSHAM 73)
Amersham (London Transport Garage)	9.00		London Transport Garage, Amersham (AMERSHAM 36)
Chalfont St. Giles	9.05		Mr. Searby, Post Office, Chalfont St. Giles (CHALFONT ST. GILES 248)
Chalfont St. Peter	9.10	6/6	Mrs. Redrup, Post Office, Chalfont St. Peter (GERRARDS CROSS 217)
Gerrards Cross	9.20		Mr. R. Binder, 6, Station Parade, Gerrards Cross (GERRARDS CROSS 406)
Uxbridge	9.30	5/-	Messrs. Garrett, 46, High Street, Uxbridge (UXBRIDGE 64)

Return fare includes admission to private enclosure near
Tattenham Corner where a view of the racing may be obtained.
Passengers board coaches near Agents' offices

LONDON TRANSPORT BELL STREET REIGATE

For Derby Day June 2nd 1937 special coaches were laid on from Chesham and
Amersham.

Image copyright TfL from the London Transport Museum collection.

Q64 operating on a 362 route. The driver on this occasion is recorded as being Tom Strictland (N7023) but one cannot be sure it is he or his conductor in this photograph taken at Frogmore Fountain, High Wycombe.
Photograph courtesy of Amersham Museum.

This is an interior view of the front of a Q-type bus, in this preserved model it can be seen the driver was separated from the passengers by a bulkhead with a door.
Photograph N Lamond.

At the end of June 1937 all drivers and conductors were briefed by the managers about the brand-new GPO (General Post Office) invention, a world first. In the event they were involved in an incident and needed to call any of the Emergency Services all they had to do was find a phone box and dial 999, this of course did not cover vehicle breakdowns!

Edward W Coleman, a bus driver from Amersham was banned from driving for six months following an accident that happened in July 1937. Edward was driving a single-decker down the road from Amersham to Chesham (then called "New Road"), he seems to have failed to see a car slowing down in front of him and only swerved at the very last minute to try and avoid hitting it. Both vehicles were badly damaged, with the car being struck by the bus and then the bus embedding itself in a residential property's front wall.

Jim was working late on 30th July 1937, so was at home that morning when an inspector called at his door, outside the house was a coach for him to drive! A train had derailed at Harrow-on-the-Hill blocking the line out to Amersham, stranding some school children who were waiting for the 9:47 train to Aylesbury; the destination at which they were due to link with an important ongoing train. The Amersham Station Master called Mr W Randall (at the bus garage) to see if he could help. Will acted immediately to get two coaches up to the station; he knew Jim would help if he was at home. The children were duly ferried to Aylesbury, arriving and holding up their connecting train by just a few minutes. How about that for service in 1937!

The very next month Albert Brown, driver of the Wrotham bound Green Line coach and his conductor Bertie Freeman had a lucky escape in White Lion Road, Amersham when a car travelling on the wrong side of that road made rather a nasty mess of the coach's offside front wing.

A rare vehicle to be seen in Chesham, this 20-seat Thornycroft Nippy JH1586 was the only vehicle of its type to operate out of Amersham. Given the fleet number NY2B it is seen here operating on the 316A route to Hemel Hempstead. The photograph is believed to be from 1938 and the vehicle was sold off very soon after it was taken.
John Hutchinson collection, no photographer credited on reverse.

"Ole Bill" the former London General "B"-type bus (seen in the next chapter) was brought out of storage in October 1937 to lead a funeral procession for James Simmonds of 13 First Avenue. James had been a driver with the old Amersham & District Company when their service comprised just two buses. His death at just 51 was a shock to all who knew him. A huge turn-out saw the procession pass from the garage down by The Crown on its way to the cemetery. The coffin bearers were conductors Hutchins, Keoline and Massey and driver Francis. Albert Brown was given the honour of driving "Ole Bill". W R Randall (District Superintendent) and G W Line (District Inspector, Amersham Depot) represented the LPTB management. James had left A&D to join the Penn Bus Company but was re-united with Amersham Garage when that business was absorbed by London Transport.

The first law ever passed in the UK to give workers formal rights to paid holiday was enacted by the Government in 1938. The "Holiday with pay Act" meant that hundreds of thousands of UK workers would be entitled to a minimum of one weeks paid holiday a year. Agricultural workers in The Chilterns would be among those to benefit and that would mean extra people taking pleasure journeys on some of the almost 100 buses now running out from Amersham garage. Also, around this time an entirely new livery started to appear as buses were refurbished. It had Lincoln green as the main colour with white window surrounds along with a white band above the lower-deck windows on double-deckers. Roofs were generally painted brown.

In February, Chittendens of Chesham started to advertise television receivers for sale or rent. If you were wealthy enough you could buy their Pye set with a 6-inch screen for 43 Guineas cash or rent it for 9 shillings a week.

21st July 1938 Dreadful Accident, three dead – Green Line driver not to blame.

Three elderly lady passengers died in this Austin car when it collided head-on with the AEC Regal T-type bus running on Green Line route B. The coach was being driven by Harold Pheby of Chesham, on route from Amersham to Aylesbury. It was close to Little Missenden when the Austin car seemed to run out of control and crossed the road. Harold swerved to the left and stopped on the verge in an attempt to avoid the oncoming car, but it was not possible. Harold said he also blew his electric horn but the car still kept coming.

Photographed by T. C. Proffitt for The Bucks Examiner, courtesy of The British Library.

Ronald Victor Redwin of Amersham, the conductor, said the coach was only doing 15 mph when he first saw the car and that was doing between 25 and 30 mph which it continued to do until impact. The coach driver was completely exonerated by the Coroner, who felt the car driver may have passed out at the wheel.

Throughout 1938 the threat of war was growing ever larger. The pressing worry was felt to be the risk of bombing raids and so local ARP warden groups were established. On Saturday 22nd October the general public will have been amazed to see searchlights illuminating the night-time sky above Chesham. This was a show put on by the Anti-Aircraft Defence Force. The Bucks Examiner reproduced a photograph showing the beams piercing the blackness and provided the caption **"All very interesting: but pray God we never have enemy aircraft here!"**

On 9th December 1938 the death of Mrs Ford from Ley Hill was reported in the Bucks Examiner. Bus drivers and conductors at the Amersham LPTB garage were saddened with this news. Mrs Ford had always invited them in when they arrived at their turnaround point of Ley Hill, she kept the kettle on the hob and they could warm their hands and feet whether it was "eight o'clock in the morning or ten-thirty at night". Mrs Ford had been ill for a year but her husband "old Joe" had carried on making the teas. For crews in the 1930's that spent waiting time down in Chesham they used the "Broadway Tea Rooms" run by Mrs Atkins, but her hours certainly weren't as flexible as Mrs Ford's in Ley Hill!

Chapter 3   Dark Days of War (1939 – 1945)

It seemed nothing short of a most horrible and frightening proposition but war seemed to be on the way. As part of preparations for a German offensive, the Chiltern towns appointed "Billeting Officers" to plan receiving evacuees from London. Amersham's was Mr A Morley-Davies; in a letter dated 20th June 1939 to the local newspaper he praised the "excellent spirit already shown" by the town's residents. A census had been taken to ascertain how many children or mother and child combinations residents could help billet. Plans were advancing, however, as the photograph below illustrates people went about their daily duties in calm and collected manner.

As mentioned in the last chapter this juggernaut from the past, looking more like a medieval siege tower, would be called out of retirement to bring a touch of nostalgia to a much-loved busman's funeral. The "Ole Bill" B43 had seen service in The Great War before returning to duties on the streets of London and then into preservation. The wreath on the upper deck (above the driver) says "Amersham" and the funeral is believed to be that of 44-year-old conductor Edward Newland in April 1939. The parade is through the streets of High Wycombe. It is probable that Will Randall is the gentleman in the light coat at the front of the cortège.
Original Photograph loaned by the Randall Family, photographer Ronald Goodearl of High Wycombe

War is Imminent!

Green Line coaches worked until the end of August 1939 and were then withdrawn. Over 400 AEC Regal T-type coaches were rapidly converted for use as public ambulances. Seating was removed and replaced with racking to provide a capacity for 10 stretchers. It was mainly anticipated these vehicles would be used to move patients out from London to country hospitals. Following some months of the period called the "phoney-war" a number of the vehicles were actually restored to passenger duties and certain Green Line routes re-instated. Some Q-type vehicles were enlisted to supplement Amersham based Green Line services up until 18th December 1940. When the attacks on London started in earnest, many T-type coaches were once again converted back to ambulance duties.

On Friday 1st September 1939, two days before war was declared, Wilf Brackley was called into the Manager's office and told he was being sent to London along with seven of his Amersham colleagues, they would be driving a selection of buses. Each was instructed to rendezvous at Albany Barracks. Wilf remembers being ticked off by his manager for forgetting his gas mask and so had to return home and collect it. He arrived at the barracks to find about 1,000 buses (this is the figure handed down in verbal accounts) parked around the square and side roads, all waiting to be called. Wilf and his mates spent a very tense weekend with little in the way of facilities and food. In fact due to Wilf having forgotten his gas mask, he was the only Amersham man who had managed to tell his wife a little of what was happening, the others had no way of contacting their families. That evening many anxious relatives turned up at the garage to find out why their loved ones had not returned from their shift. Although the drivers were not told directly, it seemed they had been requisitioned by the Army to facilitate a major troop movement. Possibly in anticipation of German bombing raids on British barracks should war be declared? The drivers were relieved on the Monday when some other colleagues from Amersham arrived; in turn they continued the wait. Wilf wearily made his way back to Amersham, sporting a weekends' growth of beard and black shadows under his eyes, he was sent home for a while as considered not presentable enough for duty; standards must not drop even in war-time.

Over the same weekend (1st – 3rd September 1939) the A41 was closed going into London to allow other London based buses to use it as a one-way street out to the country, evacuating children. Parents were expected to pay 6/- a week to the billeting family to cover some of their costs. The Bucks Examiner printed this photograph with the caption "THE OLD RED BUSES BRING IN THE EVACUEES".

The lead bus shown is 1936 built STL1165 (CLE18). It is difficult to comprehend the stress those poor little souls endured during their journey, some will be wetting themselves with fear and others showing a modicum of excitement at their first glimpses of British countryside. These initial groups came from the Ealing and Brentford areas and are outside the Thomas Harding School, Chesham. Amersham and Chesham took a greater proportion of evacuees per head of population than anywhere else in the country.

Photograph by "Graham" High Street, Chesham, published 8th September 1939, courtesy of The British Library.

1st September 1939, children crammed on the lower deck of a bus evacuating them to reach the safety of the countryside.
Image courtesy of London Transport Museum collection.

The Government had closed cinemas at the outbreak of hostilities and petrol rationing meant the private motorist was all but taken off the road. The combined effect would mean some bus services required less capacity and others more. So there begun a significant period of changing timetables and the types of buses required for their implementation.

Reservists were called up; London Transport lost 2,500 staff in the first few days of war. Their main works department at Chiswick and a number of bus and coach manufacturing outlets in and around London were turned over to producing Halifax bombers. A number of staff went from Amersham garage among them a 33-year old conductor on the Green Line service from Chesham to Oxford Circus. Mr Ernest Wilfred Battle was immediately called back to The Colours of the Durham Light Infantry and was assigned to their Army Catering Corps section. Later in the war Mr Battle was promoted to Sergeant and saw service in North Africa and Italy. His wife and two children remained at 30 Weller Road, Amersham. When interviewed towards the end of the war whilst in Italy, he said he would rather have been on the Green Line than in green Italian fields. Ernest returned to Weller Road in 1945.

Black-out precautions were introduced and these also affected the buses. Each bus had its headlamps and interior lamps shielded with black masks, restricting the light emitted and directing it downwards. White tips were painted on front mudguards and large white spots painted on the rear on every vehicle. In some cases, bus door or platform surrounds were also painted white. Vehicle windows were given a number of different treatments, some covered in mesh, some with film and some even replaced with wood. A diamond shaped "peep hole" was made in some window coverings so that passengers could peer out and identify their stop. In addition, bomb blast precautions were adopted at Amersham garage, all window glass was taped and wire mesh firmly fixed over all the glass roof lights.

This Omnibus Society photograph was taken on 16th September 1939, it illustrates some of the black-out precautions given to vehicles, painting the tips of the mudguards and placing shield covers on the headlights. These alterations would surely add to the impending fear of what war would bring. The vehicle on the left is STL1642 and to the right is six-wheeler LT1267 (behind the STL is another LT-type). LT-types had not before been seen operating on the 353 and were even more distinctive by being painted in central area red livery, the war was already altering many things. LT1267 is on this book's rear cover painting by Malcolm Drabwell.
Photograph courtesy of The Omnibus Society.

It was Monday 27th May 1940 and Jim walked down to the garage for his shift that morning. He had a horrible empty feeling in the pit of his stomach; he had just learned that his fellow driver J T Burke who joined the garage in 1935 had been "killed in action" and yesterday the King had declared it a "National day of prayer". Our soldiers in France were in "dire peril" according to the Archbishop of Canterbury, the situation seemed chaotic; Jim almost convinced himself he could hear the sound of guns booming down the London Road from the Chalfonts. Could he hear them from way over the horizon? His mind was playing tricks on him in his solitude as he paced down Stanley Hill. His bus was ready on the forecourt and Harry, his conductor waiting, they soon picked up several girls along the route all working at the new barrage balloon factory in Amersham, they seemed cheery enough as he drove up to the queue. Hadn't they heard the news, didn't they realise what was happening? Our army was defeated, the French were defeated; German jack boots would be marching here in weeks. He shivered, gave himself a shake, he needed to concentrate, there was talk of forming a group of Local Defence Volunteers at the garage and he was certainly going to join and do his bit, things looked bleak but we had beaten the Hun in 1918 so why not now? NOTE: Information regarding J T Burke comes from "Pennyfare" June 1940 P72, courtesy London Transport Museum library.

What Jim didn't know about was the secret plan, codenamed "Yellow Move". His LPTB superiors had been planning for the anticipated German invasion, at which time over 1,600 buses were going to evacuate Government personnel, over a two-day period, the plan involved bringing them all through part of the Amersham garages' operational area. Personnel and luggage were to be picked up from across London and taken to Eton Playing Fields. From there they would be divided into groups and bussed to either Slough or Beaconsfield stations for onward travel. All convoys of buses would be shadowed by a spare empty vehicle, motor-cycle mechanics, water and spares vans and a tow tractor. Nothing was left to chance and LT would provide all the necessary planning, staff and vehicles. Jim and his colleagues would have been on their list. Had the secret got out the convoys would have become a major target for the Luftwaffe but would effectively be unprotected!

As can be seen from this photograph the old A&D HQ building had been taken over to become the local "War Agricultural Office", the old A&D sheds became repair workshops for agricultural machinery.
Photograph courtesy of Amersham Museum.

"They don't like it up 'em Pike"

Originally founded in May 1940 as the Local Defence Volunteers (LDV), later renamed the "Home Guard," the Amersham Garage (London Passenger Transport Board) unit became a fairly sizeable force as the next photograph adequately shows. This was far from being the only unit in the area, but was Home Guard No. 12 platoon, part of D Company, 60th Battalion, King's Royal Rifles. It was to become a cohesive and friendly outfit with a social side admirably supported by wives and friends. All battalions and units would need to meet in some form of hall, but the LPTB lads had the largest open and ready-made covered space for miles around available to them. In all, the LPTB units of the Home Guard amounted to nearly 30,000 members across London and the Home counties.

The Amersham Garage (LPTB) Home Guard.
Back row: Not known, C. Price, F. Pearson, D. Mulkern, Not known, T. Easton, I. Hunt, A. Parrott?, A. Biddescombe, H. Vasey, A. Smith, A. Thomas?
Middle: G. Stokes, T. Oxley, not known, A. Fox, J. Hutchins, C. Bowers, F. Redding, R. F. Mayo, V. Readwin, H. Pheby
Front: Not known, Albert Robin Palser, Z. Hazel, F. Witton, Not known, W. R. Pattison, ? Marchant
Photograph John Hutchinson collection.

This photograph of STL2148 (DYL800) set to operate on Route 336 shows it newly fitted with a wartime austerity body. The vehicle was delivered in August 1937 but this low-bridge body was fitted in 1942 and the vehicle allocated to Amersham in December that year. It only remained at Amersham until July 1943. The photograph gives us a very good view on how the Works Department treated window protection and the white edging paint to aid blackout situations.
Copyright TfL from the London Transport Museum Collection.

Fares had been held unaltered from 1933 and by mid-1940 the war was causing inflation, this brought about a much-needed review on charges. Green Line increased their fares by 10%, whilst bus fares suffered a much greater percentage increase with 1d tickets going up to 1½d and 1½d tickets to 2d. Men started to be called-up or volunteered for service, however, those outside of service age continued their duties unchanged throughout the war. Laurie Akehurst's book "Country Buses Volume 1" page 107 features a lovely 1941 family photograph of driver Cecil Brown standing in front of a wartime STL running on Route 353. Photographs of wartime buses are quite rare, presumably uncomfortable questions might be asked of people walking around with cameras.

On 1st August 1940 the speed limit during black-out times was reduced from 30 mph to 20 mph. The Blitz bombing of London also commenced and it naturally caused a lot of disruption to the suburban rail network. The Ministry of War Transport decided to re-instate more of the Green Line coach network allowing a further facility for getting people in and out of London, in the main now using double-deck ST and STL vehicles. The pre-war lettering system for these routes was dropped and numbers used (see Appendix 1 pages 144-5 on routes). British Summer Time was introduced and this led to the introduction of later evening services on 305,348,353,362,394 and 397.

As wartime factory production increased, traffic on routes serving them would often necessitate the use of more or larger vehicles. The 353 serving Slough is a case in point and we can see from the photograph on page 40 the larger LT-types being put into service on this route. Tremendous pressure built up on some services and letters appeared in the press concerning the numbers of times people were left at stops as buses were full. During 1941 London Transport placed advertisements appealing to local factory bosses to try and alter starting times, as sticking with those traditionally used (e.g. on the hour or on the half hour starting times) caused so much congestion, LT suggested quarter too and past the hour starts might alleviate the problem. Gradually more routes were upgraded, on 30th April 1941 Route 305 Gerrards Cross – Chalfonts – Beaconsfield changed from being operated by Q-type single-deckers to ST-type double-deckers. Further increased capacity was at times required on Route 398A (Winchmore Hill to Amersham) and so some scheduled runnings were covered by T-type 30-seaters rather than C-type 20-seaters. Pleas were made by workers in High Wycombe that the situation to get home to places like Great Missenden at the end of a working day was so dreadful, it had been reported it could take two hours to wait to board a bus because of the queues. Reports came in that getting on a bus was becoming more a free for all than an orderly queue. LPTB were asked by the public to consider "express" buses for longer distances so the vehicles weren't full with very local passengers. The Board replied that they could not discriminate between long and short distance passengers but did appreciate the present difficulties.

The LPTB Home Guard unit were among a huge number of soldiers who formed an hour-long parade through the streets of Amersham on the evening of Tuesday 27th May 1941. It was part of a fund-raising drive for Amersham's War Weapons Week; a target of £6000 was the aim. Brazils were the major sponsors of the event. A detachment of the Royal Artillery was also in attendance with some anti-tank guns on show.

On Monday 21st July 1941 Mabel Brailsford of Amersham wrote in her diary "*The Green Line coaches are no longer running between Amersham and London – they were converted into* ambulances. *Old London buses (two-deckers) are used instead and I can travel in them with impunity, as smoking is allowed only on the upper deck and there is plenty of air in the lower. The windows however are covered in some kind of coarse green net, glued on, with only a tiny space left free. I had a front seat and could look out from behind the driver, when I raised myself on Miss Barnes' suitcase.*" Many older readers may remember the brown tobacco coloured Rexine concertina blinds that bus drivers used to shield internal light from entering their cab, it was always possible to peek through odd gaps and gain a driver's eye view of the way ahead. In Leyland Cub single-deckers a brown cloth curtain was available to pull around the driver's seat.

With many men now away fighting, staff shortages arose and women were welcomed to apply for conductor duties and even those of engineers at the garages. It was the Country Bus Service that first took on women conductors; they were issued with free uniforms but not the full green variety as sported by the men. Bus crews were expected to work a 48-hour week; however, women rose to the challenge and were quickly appointed, trained and on duty working out of Amersham. They were paid 69/9 per week rising to 81/6 with extra pay for Sundays, but as can be seen by the following two local press reports from September 1941 the job was found to be quite tough.

This photograph of an early LT conductress comes from the Amersham Museum and has been attributed to being a member of staff at the Amersham Garage.
Photograph courtesy of Amersham Museum.

Amersham conductress makes a plea

"*Will you allow me through the medium of your paper to draw attention to a condition that is causing a legitimate grievance among many bus conductresses? We are doing men's work, with as much tact and good humour as we can command, but after standing for perhaps five hours or more, naturally our energy somewhat flags, and we feel justified in sitting on the seat next to the door. However, some passengers insist on occupying this seat, even though there are other seats vacant in the bus. Many complaints have been sent in by **Joy Riders** because the conductress has requested them to take another seat, appealing to their good nature. Do you not think it is about time we worked under conditions conducive to contentment, and that a seat be reserved for conductresses on long distance journeys?*"

Opportunist local marketing rapidly comes to their aid ....

Amersham conductress knocked unconscious

Frederick Hurst was driving his bus down Ballinger Hill near Great Missenden when a Bucks Agricultural Committee van pulled out right in front of him. Frederick slammed on his brakes but his unfortunate conductress flew forward hitting her head. He got down from his cab and entered the bus to see how she was; luckily three lady passengers were giving her first aid. The police prosecuted the errant van driver who was fined £1/15/10 including costs.

Passenger numbers continued to rise and, in December 1941, double-deckers were introduced onto the 362 and 362A replacing the single-deck Qs. Routes 366 and 353 also moved over entirely to double-deckers at this time. In a further attempt to transport more people, at the end of 1941 regulations on standing passengers on conductor operated routes were relaxed such that many Q-type and T-type vehicles had all their seats removed and as many as possible re-bolted to the floor space but this time around the inner perimeter of the vehicle, thereby creating a much greater standing space in the middle aisle. The increases in carrying allowance were dramatic, a standard 30-seater T-type now carried 29 seated and up to 20 standing, the 37-seater Qs were now able to hold 33 seated and 20 standing. The squash on a full bus made for a difficult fare collecting round by the conductors but everyone was buoyed by "The Dunkirk Spirit".

This 1941 photograph is of the interior of a wartime T-type single-decker that has had its seating refitted around the perimeter of the vehicle, thus creating more standing space.
Copyright TfL from the London Transport Museum Collection.

45

Routes 348,359,397 & 398 were run by one-man-operated C-type 20-seaters due to the narrowness of the lanes around Amersham and Chesham. They were now unsuitable for the increased loading requirements of wartime. The Ministry of War Transport however, agreed to waive the no standing rule on driver only buses and from 27th April 1942 six standing passengers were allowed on the above routes.

Route 362A had been altered on 1st July 1942 when the 362 was diverted away from Ley Hill village to take more passengers on from Chesham to Berkhamsted, the 362A took its place running from Ley Hill to High Wycombe (via St. Anne's Cnr.) and the 362C was withdrawn. To save fuel and tyres, from the winter of 1942/3 no Sunday morning services would run in the Country Bus area. The North British and Merchantile Insurance Co. had relocated out of London to Newlands Park, Chalfont St Giles and was served by a special service (335A) which started on 2nd September 1942 operating out of Amersham Garage.

This wartime scene on The Broadway encapsulates much that was typical of the time. A double-deck bus with the familiar blackout white spot at the back, army lorries outside the War Agricultural Office, boiler suited personnel on the move and mothers with children, possibly evacuees. In percentage terms this area took more evacuees than any other in the country.
Image courtesy of Francis Frith collection but image held in the Bucks CC Historic Photographs collection.

On 15th September 1942, Amersham resident, Mabel Brailsford made an entry in her diary to say that blackout material in Woolworths was now 3/-, up from 1/11 last year, in Chesham she had been offered some thick black Italian cloth at a whopping 5/11. She comments that none of it will be any use when the war is over. On 18th January 1943, Mabel made a further entry about the German bombing raid on London the previous night. She felt it was a reprisal for the Allies massive raid on Berlin. She mentions she was woken at 6:00 am by the wail of the sirens that echoed from village to village and the raid on London sounds like a distant thunderstorm.

Due to the wartime shortages, bus tickets became thinner and smaller (saving on paper pulp) and now Green Line coach routes were withdrawn for a second time after Tuesday 29th September 1942. To take the place of Route 35 from Amersham to Aylesbury, Eastern National and LT jointly ran a route numbered 359. The 393 was also withdrawn.

This photograph of Bert Rogers (Dingel) was taken in the winter of 1942/3 at Amersham garage. Behind Bert is an older style AEC Regal T-type vehicle that has been converted to be a snow plough.
Photograph courtesy of A B Cross.

From 1st July 1943 Route 305A started as a special one-day service for the annual visit of relatives and friends to Chalfont Colony, this operation was repeated on 6th July 1944, 12th July 1945 and 4th July 1946, the services in 1945 and 1946 requiring Amersham to supply a double-deck vehicle.

Extra services now the Yanks are over here

In 1942/3 ninety T-type single-deckers were passed to the United States Air Force (USAF), thirty were used as personnel carriers and sixty converted to become khaki "Clubmobiles" with the American Red Cross. The "Clubmobiles" were mainly serviced at Hemel Hempstead garage but if stretched they would pass vehicles on to Amersham to maintain.

The 316 route from Chesham to Hemel Hempstead via Orchard Leigh starting using double-deck ST models from the winter of 1943/4 when the Bovingdon airbase became fully operational. Then in March 1944 the London Transport Board asked the Bucks County Surveyor and local council to further approve the use of double-deck vehicles on Routes 307 and 307A. These ran from Chesham, through Lye Green to the USAF base at Bovingdon. There was no objection to the request. At the same time requests were also put in to formalise, with the erection of concrete post and "Bus Stop" signs, a number of stopping places in and around Chesham. Not all were approved but the number of "recognised" stopping places increased soon afterwards.

The ringing of church bells had been banned since the outbreak of war unless we were being invaded; although the 1942 victory at Alamein had seen some local churches ring theirs. Finally, in April 1943 this ban was lifted and the Chilterns once again relished hearing the peals from its old churches.

This photograph inside a converted AEC Regal T-type vehicle shows it being used by the USAF as a food and drink mobile vending operation. Known as "Clubmobiles" these converted coaches offered much needed refreshments to the service men. This is an original official postcard passed by the U.S. censors, it has the written addition indicating the card depicts a scene at Bovingdon USAF base, this is repeated on the reverse. Also, on the reverse is printed "No stamp required if sent by members of the U.S. Armed Forces" and "Red Cross Clubmobiles staffed by American Girls bring coffee and doughnuts to U.S. Forces overseas." The card dates to 1943-4.
John Hutchinson collection.

Due to the continued fuel and rubber shortages London Transport took steps to prevent buses stopping and starting more than was absolutely necessary. Advertisements placed in 1943 stated that by June, "buses would have to be requested to stop at designated "Bus Stop Request" points only. At night passengers were asked to either hold out something "white" or if carrying a torch, hold out one hand and point your torch downwards to illuminate your hand as the bus approached. Never flash the torch at a bus driver".

It was clear that as war dragged on, London Transport struggled to meet demand and offer the type of service to which the public had become accustomed. During 1944 they put out a number of somewhat apologetic advertisements, the following appeared in the Bucks Examiner in March:-

"LONDON TRANSPORT STILL SERVING MILLIONS – London Transport is a public service vital to the community. In war, as in peace, its resources are devoted to meeting the travel needs of London's millions. The inevitable shortage of labour and materials, the blackout, the growing age of vehicles, and many other problems, condition resources in war. Nevertheless, the essential needs of London's millions are still being met by London Transport day in and day out even in this fifth year of war."

Two weeks later they followed up with this advertisement:-

"LONDON TRANSPORT STILL SERVING MILLIONS – War conditions have imposed restrictions on London Transport. But by adjustments to services to overcome the fuel problem, by the sacrifice of spit and polish, by the use of substitutes to replace materials in short supply, by the cheerful co-operation of the public and by a loyal staff, London Transport is enabled to meet the essential needs of London's millions in this fifth year of war."

Not only were serviceable vehicles in short supply but so were staff and Amersham garage placed this advertisement in the local press at the end of March 1944. It seems that there were Ministry of Labour restrictions on employing younger women; presumably they were required for more labour-intensive work. In 1943 LT were still offering women a starting weekly wage of 69/9 (£3/9/9) rising to 81/6 (£4/1/6), unchanged from 1941.

Unusual advert placed by local opticians Turner & Browning.

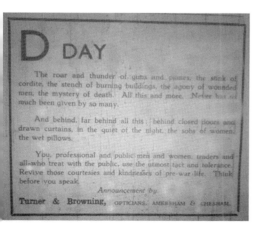

This advertisement appeared in the Bucks Examiner on 9th June 1944 (immediately after D-Day), it contains an interesting message. This was not an isolated advert of its type from these opticians, others that followed made similar profound statements about the time and events. The company was still trading in Chesham in 2017.

LT's problems reach boiling point in Chesham – An agonised Bellingdon lady protests.

On July 22nd 1944 a sad situation caused an incident to flare up on Chesham Broadway when Maud Page of Bellingdon jumped a bus stop queue of about 50 people to get on the last bus to her village. She then emphatically refused driver/conductor David Bailey's demands leave his bus. Ms Page said to him "I'm here and here I will stay," at this point she sat down in his driver's seat and started singing and bouncing up and down. The bus was due to leave for Buckland Common at 7:55 p.m. it was full, including six standing, and was considerably delayed by the fracas. Mr Bailey phoned for the police and the lady was charged with disorderly behaviour and refusing to leave a public vehicle when requested. Maud Page was found guilty on both counts and fined 20/- for each offence.

Pressure on bus services was such that travel not related to the war effort was discouraged. The advertisement on the left had been placed in the Bucks Examiner the previous month and shows how seriously they took the burgeoning situation. Posters such as the one on the right would also appear on buildings.

By September residents all along Route 397 from Chesham to Tring via Hawridge and Wigginton were up in arms about their poor service frequency as well as the state of the roads. They knew that the same was true for routes out to The Chalfonts and to Watford, people left behind during the day and worse still after the last bus. LPTB ran advertising campaigns urging people not to leave their journeys until the last bus, but it seems from press reports that the people trying for the last one had already been passed by previous full buses. Such was the ferocity of the residents that a 359-signature petition was sent to London Transport. LPTB Public Relations Officer Mr F Scothorne replied assuring them that a new timetable was under construction and would be implemented by the end of the month or very early in October. The Company stuck to their word and services on that route were increased but problems were not resolved. By December Mr G F Sharp, the Rector of Hawridge and Cholesbury and also the Vicar of St. Leonards pleaded that they now had an over-supply at certain times on Route 397 and could those crews be directed to create a service between Buckland Common and St. Leonards?

The Amersham Garage (LPTB) Home Guard Social Club had opened their winter season on 8th September 1944 with a concert followed by a dance. There was good attendance of members and friends. Sgts. Fry and Edmunds played accordions and Cpls. Rutherford and Sargent performed sketches and songs. "The dance that followed went merrily until a late hour" reported the Bucks Examiner. Like all other units in the area this section of the Home Guard was officially stood down in December, however, the social side of things for the employees went on much as before, such was the camaraderie amongst the staff.

More staff had come forward.

Following the March recruitment drive, more women had applied and were trained as conductors to work in the Amersham area. Their long sacrifice was given public recognition, as by September 1944 letters started to appear in the local papers showing great concern for women who were having to start shifts as early as 5:57 a.m. and how they were travelling 3 or 4 miles to even get to work. Surely the LPTB could provide a staff bus was the clarion call of the correspondents? The following (abbreviated account) came from Rosemary Blatchford, "Due to their physical make-up how could these girls be expected to walk or cycle that distance, do a full day up and down stairs on a bus, then go shopping and do housework?"

Mr H V Willoughby, Branch Secretary for the Amersham (Busman's) branch of the TGWU responded to the calls with thanks and a heart rending piece acknowledging the suffering they were enduring, at times in weather "unfit for animals", but he assured the public, the Union was still "trying to obtain a staff bus, through the proper Trade Union channels".

Army Jeep takes a direct hit near the Amersham Garage

Frank Mayo, a coach driver with LPTB was cycling along the London Road, Amersham on 24th November, as he neared its junction with Station Road he saw an Army Jeep turn left from Station Road and head towards Chalfont St. Giles. Frank then saw a lorry travelling on the wrong side of the road, it drove straight into the front of the Jeep. The lorry driver said he didn't see the Army vehicle, the damage caused was considerable. Mr Mayo gave evidence in court and the lorry driver was fined £3 and his licence endorsed for "careless driving".

As 1944 came to a close, hard pressed garage staff were given some light relief as no bus services were scheduled to run on Christmas Day.
The Hoover Company even got in on the act and placed this well-timed advertisement in the Bucks Examiner – somewhat patronising by today's standards.

Hoover advertisement, local press 1944.

1945 - Proud victory parades and recognition for all Civil Defence services

Across London and the Home Counties, London Transport and its staff had certainly "done their bit" for the war effort. They had kept a transport network working when at times it seemed impossible to cope. They had provided shelter for thousands in the London Underground. Their staff had helped build 400 Halifax bombers, made thousands of munitions and repaired vital motors and tanks. Their service lorries had pulled vehicles from bomb craters and cleared roads as well as their Home Guard units who had protected the civilian population.

On Saturday 12th May 1945 after Victory in Europe had been proclaimed, an Amersham Council Victory Assembly was called for, all local Home Guard members and anyone wishing to attend was asked to parade in uniform at 16:30 hours at Rectory Barn (11th Bucks Battalion HQ). The very next Saturday an even bigger parade was held at the Grammar School playing field, all Civil Defence services were invited. The Home Guard, Police, ARP, Nursing Services, National Fire Service and ATC attended. Many dignitaries addressed the assembly praising them, saying "their task was done", they had the sincere "gratitude of the citizens of Amersham", for the devoted and efficient manner they had so loyally and "unselfishly carried out their duties throughout the five and half years of war". Through all the trial and danger that ensued. Praise too was given to those responsible for billeting arrangements, the WVS and staff of the Food Office. The assembly was reminded that, at its height, 21,000 evacuees had been billeted in our area, increasing the population by 63%. This was a greater increase than in any other district in the country and everyone should be proud of how they had coped and how smoothly and efficiently they had made the transitions. This parade was described by the speakers as the last one, a farewell to civil defence in the area and a job well done.

On 29th June 1945 some interesting facts emerged concerning actual activities in the area, with which the Civil Defence services would have had direct involvement. This data was released by Mr W G Garrett-Pegge, Sub-Controller Civil Defence Services No. 5 Area, which was based in Chesham and covered Amersham and Beaconsfield. During the time of hostilities:-
227 alerts were received.
First alert: 7:30 a.m. 6th September 1939 – probably a false alarm.
First major alert: 12:56 a.m. 25th June 1940.
Last alert: 8:58 a.m. 29th March 1945.
Longest alert: lasted 13 hours on 11th December 1940, sirens went off nightly at this time.
91 separate incidents of enemy bombing were reported.
279 High explosive bombs were dropped on the area, 8 flying bombs.
5 parachute mines, 29 oil bombs, 25 incendiary bombs.
9 fatalities recorded, 30 people more or less seriously injured.

A final letter of thanks to those local civil defence units was sent to the Bucks Examiner at this time and concluded thus "Whatever trials face us in winning the peace, you can, one and all, feel justly proud in the knowledge, that through your steadfastness, patience and devotion to duty, you have done your share in helping our gallant Forces and Allies to win the war".

With the end of hostilities during the summer of 1945, the Government needed to restore the country to a peace time footing in the shortest timescale. However, it was six months before a full fuel provision was returned to London Transport and it could, in turn, make necessary adjustments to its services. The numbers of passengers carried had almost doubled during the war years. With so many factors having contributed; troop movements, private car usage curtailment, increased factory output and general population movement it was certainly going take a period of time to settle down and allow the planners at LT to match services to demand. In May 1939 only six double-deck vehicles (ST-types) operated out of Amersham by July 1945 this had figure had risen to about 26 double-deckers (16 x STL; 10 x ST). On 4th July 1945, two months after VE Day, increased bus services and later evening runs were introduced on 305, 335, 336, 353, 362/A and 394. Also, on 17th October 1945 Sunday morning services were re-introduced on 335, 336, 353 and 362 at the same time the Newland Park 353A was withdrawn, things were getting back to normal. The North British Insurance Co. had returned to its London premises.

Peace across the world but unrest at the Amersham Garage

The bus fleet was generally worn out, through lack of maintenance and replacement and with some surprise the attraction of employment as bus drivers and conductors had diminished from the pre-war era. The Garage now had the requirement for around 150 drivers and 100 conductors. Prior to war a job with London Transport had been seen as a well-paid and regarded occupation, this vision had not withstood the intervening six years. Wages in the industry had been kept down whilst war-time inflation had eroded their spending power, leading to it being a far less attractive employment prospect by the end of 1945. Dissatisfaction spread throughout the country bus staff, none more than at Amersham. By October 1945 the Union was voicing the staff unrest to management and the threat of a strike loomed. Staff had hoped that their workload would ease with the ending of the war; however, they felt the opposite was taking place. They were upset with new Sunday working arrangements and accused management of employing plain clothes men and women to spy on them when they were at home or off sick. They were unhappy with suffering loss of pay for the most minor of infringements. Drivers particularly felt 5-6 hours continuous duty without a break was too excessive and injurious to health. Additionally, although they were grateful to have 12 days paid holiday a year they were so restricted to when they could take it, sometimes only in winter, which they never really gained much benefit from it. Finally, if they were off on Christmas Day the Company counted that as their day off for the week, so was not paid. Contemporary reports indicate the Amersham staff took limited strike action and thanked the public for their understanding. The matter then went to further negotiations between the Union and LPTB. Certainly, all was not well on the Amersham buses.

It is possible that the dissatisfaction felt amongst staff caused them to try and earn some extra money by devious means. John Hutchinson (an employee at Amersham from 1971) recalls handed down reports about shifting STLs between garages at night to earn a bit more overtime.

Before we leave this chapter, there is one very early memory to pass on from the granddaughter of Will Randall. Janet remembers, at the age of 6 (1945) her mother putting her on a London Transport bus in Marlow and entrusting her safe passage to the driver. She was destined to get to the Amersham Bus Garage where Will worked as Regional Manager. On the journey she felt very sick and had to ask the driver to stop. Passengers complained that they needed to get on but the driver supported her and said "he would be in trouble with the boss if he didn't help her out and see her safely to the bus garage". He kept his promise to her mother and she was delivered safely but later confided she didn't know what a "boss" was!

Chapter 4   Post War – The Golden Era (1946 –1954)

With the war now behind them, the management wanted to see the country bus scene returning to some sort of pre-war normality. Green Line routes dropped their pre-war route letters and adopted a new numbering system. The first post-war coach route from Amersham started running on 3rd April 1946, numbered the 703 it ran from Amersham to Wrotham and offered an hourly service, timetabled to get to London in 50 minutes (four coaches were based at Amersham and three at the other end, Swanley). The Chesham to Oxford Circus service was reinstated on 16th June 1946 as Route 725, also requiring seven coaches. There now began what was later to be appreciated as the "Golden Era" for country bus and coach travel. Private cars were still a luxury that few could justify but people yearned to experience the new post conflict freedom of movement. Lots of factories had sprung up outside the Capital and there was two-way traffic for people from the inner city visiting old friends who had relocated to the country.

The main black-out precautions at the garage had been removed some while ago with the exception of the wire mesh below the roof lights. In-house service staff now took this down and there was a free-for-all to take it home for chicken coups, allotments and the like. That was until the garage received a phone call from H.O. to say that they planned to remove it in a few weeks' time. Luckily most was retrieved and handed to the appropriate staff when they arrived, they were probably grateful their job had been done for them!

London Transport now started promotional adverts for Country Bus travel. The first I have come across in the Bucks Examiner during 1946 sought to attract visitors to Whipsnade Zoo. It involved a somewhat contorted and time sapping journey from either Amersham or Chesham to Rickmansworth (336), then take the 321 to St. Albans and then a 368 to the Zoo.

This 1946 photograph of Green Line T458, registration no. ELP182, waiting at Amersham Garage was taken in the early months of Route 703 operation after the war. This vehicle had been requisitioned in September 1939 and used as an ambulance throughout the hostilities. It underwent a refurbishment in March 1946 to facilitate its return to passenger duties. It is finished in green and white livery.
Photograph courtesy of A B Cross.

November 1946 and a lady, complete with wicker shopping basket, boards the 348 at Tring. Leyland Cub C41 is operating out of Amersham. The sign on the rear nearside panel reads "*Courtesy and Service*".
Image courtesy of TfL from the London Transport Museum collection.

An interior view of a 20-seat Leyland Cub looking towards the rear. The long seats at the rear must have formed a nice gossip area!
Photograph N Lamond.

Since 1934 London Transport had aspired to standardising its fleet but a lack of vehicles during the war continued to thwart their plans. Here we see a very old looking bus running in Chesham on Route 362 to Ley Hill. The photograph was probably taken shortly after the war. ST1054, registration GO654 is an AEC Regent vehicle which dates from 1931, it seated 49 passengers and had a staircase that went up one third of the way into the saloon, the blanked-out window indicates its position. The entrance platform was at the rear. It stayed in service until September 1949.

This original photograph has no credit on the reverse and is in the John Hutchinson collection.

War-Time Hero back to work at Amersham Garage

On Tuesday 23rd July 1946, Amersham Garage employee, Mr Malcolm Melton was presented to His Majesty King George VI at Buckingham Palace. Receiving the Distinguished Conduct Medal awarded for "conspicuous bravery", when as a paratrooper in 1942 he had landed in Jugoslavia (sic). Mr Melton from Winchmore Hill, was demobbed in the rank of Company-Sergeant-Major, 101st Special Service Squadron, General Staff Intelligence.

At the end of 1946 the Amersham branch Sports & Social Club held a special dinner at The Millstream to celebrate the return of staff that had fought in the war. Don Edwards' invitation is shown below.

The Committee and Members of the

AMERSHAM LONDON TRANSPORT SPORTS CLUB
(Country Buses)

request the pleasure of the Company of

MR. DON: EDWARDS
at a

DINNER

to celebrate the return of Staff who served in H.M. Forces

1939—1946, at the "Millstream," Amersham, on Tuesday,

17th December, 1946, 7 for 7.30 p.m.

R.S.V.P. not later than   A. W. HUTCHINS, Hon. Sec.,
December 7th, 1946.   L.P.T.B. Garage, Amersham.

Image from John Hutchinson collection.

For Christmas Day 1946 both London Country buses and Green Line coaches ran services all day on their major routes. This meant the 335, 336, 353, 362 would now run until 4:00 p.m. on Christmas Day, a schedule that would continue until 1951.

On the 3rd January 1947 a detailed article concerning the increased demand on bus services appeared in The Bucks Free Press. The report was based on information direct from LPTB who recognised the demands for its services. It stated that every available vehicle was at work and since the end of the war an additional 600 buses were in service across the network. Traffic was at a higher level than at any time in the history of London Transport; as many as 15,000,000 passengers had been carried in a single day.

The Board said it had placed additional vehicle orders with manufacturers but delivery schedules were very slow. Unlike the end of the First World War when nearly all soldiers were demobbed instantly, this time release back to civilian life was phased, in a bid to help the economy develop a measured return to normality. Britain started a big drive to sell home produced goods around the world and that certainly boosted employment levels. In addition, there was a demand for recreational travel, people wanted to get out into the country for fresh air and leisure. The Chilterns, with its close proximity to a bombed-out London, will have seemed a world away for a journey taking only 60 minutes. Our local bus network would benefit greatly from these visitors; it could transport them down the country lanes, dropping them near footpaths for strolls across fields and woods, down green valleys, alongside streams and to picturesque villages. There could be no greater nor inexpensive pleasure so near to north-west London. However, from reading a 1946 book called "Chiltern Footpaths" by Annan Dickson one might get the impression some visitors looked down their noses at the locals, I quote from one passage on page 15 "One word of warning to the seeker after rural "characters". Man goes about his labours in the Chilterns not to provide entertainment for "foreigners", but because it is his job. For the most part he is a brisk worker, with scant inclination to dally in conversation; you must take him as you find him".

To cope with passenger demand the Amersham garage desperately needed to recruit staff and among others, William Thomas Samuel Perren (Bill) successfully applied to become a conductor. His wartime work had been making bombs in a factory at Bourne End (near Marlow). Bill and his new wife, Winifred, rented a place at Lee Common as Bill was about to start on a chapter of his life that would take him through to retirement some 40 years later. We will pick up on Bill a few times as our story continues. Don Pearce also joined as a conductor after the war; like Bill, Don went on to become a driver and was recognised in 1986 for attaining 34 years free from accidents. He put it down to 90% luck, but also said he followed the advice an old driver gave him as he started this career "never hurried, never worried yet still usually arrived on time, giving everyone a nice ride". Don would finally retire in 1987 after 41 years' service. Other joiners immediately after the war, who went on to give very long service included Bill Holland, James Lambourne, Bill Grafton, Ken Parker and Frank Onions. All joining around this time and were to embark on a journey that would speed towards a much-altered future. Some of these staff would be new to the Chilterns and certainly unfamiliar with the still often heard broad South Buckinghamshire accents. A conductor being asked for a ticket to Chezzum might struggle somewhat. The locals also had a habit of ignoring "t's" in certain words, so in conversation you might hear "ahh a grea place for cachin rabbuhs all abou yeer". I'll leave you to work it out. Even John Hutchinson, starting out in the early 1970s commented "I found some *of the schoolgirls getting on my bus seemed to want "sex" when it transpired they wanted a "6" fare".* Ha-ha; still John was young and impressionable then!

Her last bus . . .

An accident that proved fatal outside The Hen and Chickens, Botley.

On January 13th 1947, 82-year old Mr Walter Child from Botley House, Botley Road was waiting for a bus to take him down into Chesham, he was temporarily sheltering from the wind in the entrance to the Hen and Chickens pub. Mr Child was blind in one eye but saw the bus coming along and, without properly checking traffic, ran across the road to meet it. Unfortunately, his sprint made him collide with the side of a passing car. Whilst the accident only occasioned him a broken leg, he subsequently contracted pneumonia in hospital and died as a result. The Coroner recorded a death by "Misadventure". Some locals called for a bus shelter to be erected opposite the pub. As can be seen from the 1947 advertisement above, put out by The Ministry of Transport, this was an all too regular occurrence with traffic numbers increasing and the public awareness of danger not keeping pace with the change.

Could one wish for a more nostalgic photograph? Trolleybus wires, old police box, mother with period pram and a Q-type coach travelling through Ealing on its way out to Amersham on Green Line Route 725. The date is 20th August 1947, vehicle Q222.
Image courtesy of TfL from the London Transport Museum collection.

Garage electrician Bert Chennery who had started working at Amersham in 1935 recalled some handling problems on the Q-type vehicles. In wet weather and especially when encountering tram tracks in London, the single rear wheels apparently made them feel a little skittish. Records still held at Acton, show 49 different Q-types worked out of Amersham before, during and after the war. Although the number post 1945 was very small as T-types were the preferred choice. It is amazing that such a high number are recorded when almost no photographs captured their presence in the Amersham area.

On 29th January 1947 the temperature fell to -16 degrees centigrade in some places. Heavy snowfalls caused chaos and a thaw only came in late March.

A crystal kingdom with trees sparkling as if dressed with tinsel, the children jumped for joy but the bus drivers struggled on against the odds. This Leyland Cub, working out of Amersham shows the difficulties encountered in the harsh winter of 1947.
Photograph courtesy of Michael Baker collection, London Bus Museum.

Tribute to Bus Men

This letter appeared in The Bucks Examiner on 7th February 1947 under the above title.

"Sir – May a regular traveller on the 362 route offer his thanks to the bus men for the magnificent job they have done in running almost continuously and to schedule in the recent appalling weather and road conditions? I would take my hat off to them if I possessed one.
F H R Aldred, Seven Firs, Watched Lane, Holmer Green."

Despite petrol still being rationed in 1947, LT launched new timetables for later in the year; they provided a Sunday morning service on Route 305 and afternoon and evening services on Routes 335, 336 and 353. These would allow far greater opportunities for both tourists and locals to visit the Chiltern beauty spots and places like Windsor.

Those Yanks and their big cars, they could get petrol!

In May 1947 Charles Vincent Weller a mobile LPTB inspector was travelling on his motorbike between Chalfont St. Giles and Amersham. As he got to the "Mill Stream" a large American Buick car passed him so closely that it caught his coat and ripped it, Charles narrowly averted crashing. He regained control and pursued the offender whom he could not catch but was able to note his registration. He reported the offence to the police and PC Border prosecuted the driver who, in court, swore that he was totally unaware of catching Mr Weller's coat. The Bench accepted that the defendant's car was the "culprit" but held that the defendant had no knowledge of the accident and dismissed the case.

As mentioned in the last chapter, some staff had not been particularly happy at the Amersham Garage and this was to continue. With factories having returned to a 5-day week, bus crews felt they too should share in a reduced workload. They were currently working 48-hour weeks with one day off in every eight. The buses themselves were worked hard, operating for 16-hours a day on weekdays and 14-hours most Sundays. Passenger numbers were very high and crews seldom allowed any part of a weekend off. Their pleas did not go unheard and the Board reduced hours to 44 per week from 29th October 1947. Following this change, Route 725 (Chesham-London) was withdrawn and Route 709 (from Godstone) extended to Amersham and Chesham. Route 710 from Crawley was likewise extended to Amersham as well. After this, routes and timetables generally settled down for the next four years.

From the beginning of 1948 the operations controlled by the London Passenger Transport Board were handed over to the London Transport Executive (LTE), accordingly over the next few months, this change was reflected in the wording on the lower sides of the vehicles.

A rare photograph indeed taken inside the Amersham Garage on 14th February 1948. The old looking double-decker was on loan to the garage to act as a trainer instruction unit for the new RT Class double-deckers that would be arriving soon. The trainer vehicle was an RT chassis carrying an old Tilling ST body. Alongside it is T667 registration no. EYK302 with blind set for service on Route 394c, this vehicle had only recently been converted back to 34 seats from having wartime perimeter seating (30-seats and 20-standing).
Photograph courtesy of the A B Cross collection.

Leyland Cub on Route 397 to Tring is hit by a lorry

Robert S Ferby of London Road, Amersham was driving his LT Leyland Cub along The Vale, Chesham operating on Route 397 on 18th August 1948. As he approached the entrance to Vale

Farm he saw a lorry coming fast in the opposite direction, for safety purposes he pulled over and was stationary when the vehicle got alongside him. However, the lorry still struck the side of his bus. The lorry driver was prosecuted for "driving without due care and attention" and the Bench fined him £3 and endorsed his licence.

Some at Amersham Garage see red!

A report in the Bucks Examiner for December 1948 follows a letter arriving at their offices from Mr H V Willoughby of the Amersham Busman's Branch of the Transport and General Workers Union, he states "by a very large majority that a member that was connected with any Communist organisation shall not be permitted to hold office in the branch". Mr Wilfred Saint, Garage Representative and Delegate had further written to say that Mr Willoughby was not an official of the Branch and his letter was premature, he accepted he was one of the Communists concerned and so was Brother Haines (Section Secretary) but the constitution of the Union was to embrace people of different persuasions and religious affiliations and the basis of Trade Unionism was unity, so we need compromise on these matters. The constitution stated "people should be elected to office on merit" and at a later "Special Meeting" the members agreed to uphold that point. It therefore seemed that although the issue rumbled on for a while longer, reds were not getting a clear green light at Amersham.

The garage was being hit by two shortages at this stage, one of staff and the other of serviceable vehicles. There were a number of reasons for staff shortages; competition was now fierce from our manufacturing and service industries and housing accommodation prices were on the rise. Ronald Bovingdon (senior) joined in 1948 as a driver on 5/11/- for a 44-hour week. In addition, and as already mentioned, new vehicles had been extremely slow to come from manufacturers. Between December 1948 and February 1950, ten Bristol K6A-type lowbridge double-deckers that had been destined for Hants and Dorset Bus Company were temporarily diverted to the London Country Area. Amersham was among the garages to benefit from using a few of these on Route 336. They carried Hants and Dorset bonnet numbers prefixed "TD" but had London Transport emblems attached to their radiators. The vehicles stayed in London Country service until transferred to their rightful owner in March 1950. An example of one of these vehicles (TD893) is shown on page 65.

MEN AND WOMEN
CONDUCTORS WANTED
IN THE AMERSHAM AREA
APPLY TO YOUR LOCAL EMPLOYMENT EXCHANGE

This advertisement is exhibited with the permission of the Ministry of Labour and National Service under the Control of Engagement Order

A 1949 London Transport recruitment poster specifically designed for the Amersham area. It seems that the garage was particularly short of conductors. Fortunately, some Amersham based buses were already one man operated but the conductors that were employed were now having to work weekends off and extra hours during the week to cope. Women were certainly still welcome to apply for the jobs, a far cry from attitudes before the war.
Image courtesy of TfL from the London Transport Museum collection.

A 1949 photograph taken on the Broadway Chesham. The 20-seater one-man operated diesel engined Leyland Cub C39 registration no. BXD664 working Route 348 returning back via Bellingdon. This vehicle had only recently come to work at the Amersham Garage and it remained there until withdrawal from service in December 1953. These Cubs were fitted with Short Brother's bodies a company better known for producing aircraft. They were small manoeuvrable vehicles highly suited to Buckinghamshire country lanes and serving our small villages.
Photograph taken by John C Gillham, courtesy A B Cross.

Chesham Broadway in July 1949, T624 is working the pretty Route 394B running out to Chartridge and Ballinger. (Right) an interior shot from this type of vehicle showing detailing and clock mounted on the bulkhead behind the driver's cab.
Photograph courtesy of the A B Cross collection.

An interesting nearside view of a 48-seat country STL-type vehicle with front entrance, photograph taken on 5th October 1949. This 1935 built STL 1019 (BLH876) is seen set for Route 353 to Berkhamsted Station. No door was fitted to this style of country bus and despite a carefully angled bulkhead panel, winter draughts were not appreciated by most passengers.
Photograph courtesy of A B Cross.

This 1942 built vehicle with increased seating for 56 on a longer chassis is STL 2669, shown here on route 362A to Ley Hill. Only a handful of buses were actually built during the war as factory output was dedicated to the war effort. As a consequence, this bus had a very austere interior with wooden framed seats, no panelling and a minimum of opening windows. The photograph was taken on October 5th 1949, this vehicle only worked out of Amersham garage for a short time. It displays the newly introduced post-war green and cream livery. It was withdrawn from passenger service in 1952 and after a period as a staff bus, LT converted it to a service vehicle lorry (1017J) and it then stayed on until 1965. The RTs were set to takeover.
Photograph courtesy of A B Cross.

The STL class was actually initially released shortly after the ST class but LT had inherited lots of those in takeovers and so the STLs made a slower entrance. The STLs were diesel engined buses that made them less costly to run. Like all double-deckers before them the poor driver wasn't provided with a door to keep out the cold and certainly no heater!

A column in the Bucks Examiner reported on the LT Amersham Garage for the 1949 North-West Area of London Transport Country Buses Safe Driver Awards as follows:-
"It is interesting to note that those who have known this garage from the old days of the A&D - the local bus service - that many of the old A&D men of those days figure in the 1949 awards, and those that receive the 11-14 years Oak Leaf Bars will recall the old days and their merry events inseparable from a pioneer service. Some of those men of the old days have gone, alas, and this list inevitably recalls them.

J C Archer, W J Brackley, W A Brown, W J Chapman, W M Dyer, E W J Easton, B W Francis, A Gurney, A W Harrowell, T Hoard, J Machin, D H Mulkern, W R Pattison, R A Richardson, T F Stictland and R W Walton".
"5-year Medal - E J Revel."

It was now 16 years since the "old A&D" had been taken over but the firm's memory still lingered with staff.

Accidents involving buses in and around the hamlet of Ley Hill were probably quite rare, although the pages of this book and its predecessor do record some. On the evening of Saturday 23rd April 1950 Mr Ronald Shilton of Redhill Street, London clearly had not understood the bus driver's intention to turn around in front of The Swan public house. This manoeuvre was normal at Ley Hill Common, but Mr Shilton proceeded with an overtaking move and thus collided with the side of the bus. He was taken to Amersham General Hospital where he was detained with leg injuries. Buses only had side trafficator arms at this time and drivers felt hand signals were far more obvious, although maybe not in this case.

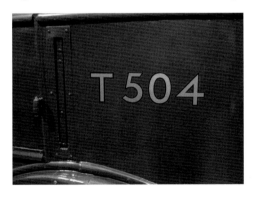

The trafficator arm casing can be clearly seen in this photograph of T504.

Getting on and off these older style buses was also not without its dangers. On 23rd August, Mrs A Humphrey of 75 Vale Road, Chesham came a cropper when stepping off a London Transport bus outside the Salvation Army Hall on Berkhampsted Road, Chesham, she fell and also ended up as an inpatient at Amersham General Hospital with injuries to her leg and wrist.

Chesham Broadway as the decade nears its end, on 5th October 1949 an old and a new double-decker are operating on Route 336 to Watford. Top: is a new Bristol K6A-type, TD893 on loan to London Transport due to a shortage of vehicles. Bottom: the 1930 built ST141, still operating with its old petrol engine, it was converted to diesel before the year was out and remarkably stayed in service until 1952. Both vehicles have low height bodies to go under Blackhorse Bridge Amersham. The driver of the new vehicle now has a door!

Both photographs courtesy of A B Cross collection.

Traversing the railway bridge adjacent to High Wycombe station. STL 2674 on Route 362B is arriving at High Wycombe coming down the hill from Hazelmere. The cyclists starting the upward trek typify a period for many workers from the 1930s to the 1950s. This shot was taken on 30th May 1950 and the vehicle was operating out of High Wycombe garage. FXT397 was another that had been built in 1942 to wartime austerity standards, it was initially painted in central area red with a brown roof. By 1944 it was given its green livery, a colour in which it remained until disposal in June 1958. It spent its last six years as a staff bus working from LT's Aldenham Works. For many years it had been a rule that only "crash gearbox" vehicles were allowed to operate on this hill as it had been found too steep for early pre-selector boxes to handle.
Photograph courtesy A B Cross collection.

GREEN LINE embark on big sales drive

Throughout 1950/1, GREEN LINE coaches massively promoted their operations from the area. Small display advertisements, specially drawn for each event would appear almost monthly in the local press. Here are some of the events advertised around this time.

2 June 1950 – See Trooping the Colour travel by Green Line
30 June 1950 – Tercentenary Parade of The Coldstream Guards go by Green Line
15 Sept 1950 – Go to Beckonscot from Amersham for just 8d single
30 Sept 1950 – Go and support QPR v Grimsby on the Green Line
13 October 1950 – Visit The Motor Show at Earls Court, just 3/3 by Green Line from Chesham
9 November 1950 – The Lord Mayor's Show, price now 3/7 from Chesham (single)
26 December 1950 – Chelsea v Portsmouth at Stamford Bridge
1-13 January 1951 – Schoolboys' Exhibition
April 1951 – Visit the Festival of Britain by Green Line
June 1951 – See the Royal Tournament at Earls Court, price from Chesham 3/3

21-26 June 1951 – Lords Test Match, England v S Africa, price from Chesham 3/4.

Around this time Margaret Johnson, who lived in Latimer, recalls trips to see Wembley ice-hockey and Christmas Ice Shows – catching the midnight coach from Wrotham and walking down Stony Lane at around 2:00 am in the morning to get home!

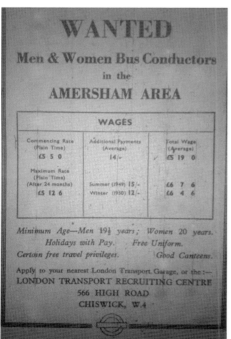

Advert September 1950

Bill Perren had joined Amersham garage as a conductor shortly after the war and hadn't found it easy to get accommodation close to the garage. He eventually managed to get a pre-fab on White Lion Road (pre-fabs were rapidly constructed single story dwellings built in the early post-war years). Bill, Winifred and family moved into 31 St. Georges on 1st October 1950, it became their pride and joy for a number of years. The rent was 16/1 per week and the rates 5/11. Bill's gross pay at this time was £5/12/6 a week.

The need to operate "lowbridge" buses under Amersham's Black Horse Bridge could not be more apparent than in this shot taken on 22nd October 1950. The old chap with his flat cap looks on in seeming amazement; one can almost hear him saying "will it get under?" These were the long awaited new vehicles that would release the loaned Bristols and let them get off to the deprived Hants & Dorset bus company. RLH 1, KYY501 was only a matter of months old when this lovely time capsule of a photograph was taken. She was operating on Route 336 and stayed working out of Amersham for 5 years. By the end of 1956 she was painted red and did some work on the 230 route in the Kenton area of Middlesex. She finally left London Transport at the end of 1964.
Photograph taken by J C Gillham.

Former long-term Hemel Hempstead resident Jennifer Worth who recorded her 1950s work experiences in the book "Call the Midwife" (made into a very popular BBC television series) wrote of her enjoyment of double-deck bus travel at this time.

"I have always loved the top front seat of a London bus, and to this day I maintain that no transport, however expensive or luxurious, can possibly offer half so much by way of scenery, advantaged viewing point and leisurely locomotion. There is endless time to absorb the passing scenes, perched high above everyone and everything".

This 1951 photograph shows 3-year old AEC Regal T-type (T791) picking up passengers on Chesham's Broadway, having come down on Route 394A from Ballinger Village. It was originally painted green and white but is seen here having just been refinished in green with a cream waist line. This vehicle was withdrawn from Amersham Garage and LT service in July 1958.
Photograph courtesy of A B Cross collection.

Jim was sad about the news that fellow Amersham Driver Stanley Francis had passed away in July 1951. It was a wonderful tribute to his service that the WW1 bus called "Ole Bill" would be detailed to precede the hearse and mourners from the Garage to the Amersham burial ground. The Superintendent and Chief Inspector were there, as well as good old Mr Randall who had employed Jim 26 years earlier. It was also the year in which Jim had bought his first ever car, a Standard 9 that Vi and he named "Betsy". She was a pre-war "sit-up-beg" model on large but extremely narrow wire wheels. Jim had been driving the local buses for so long now, he felt he knew everybody as most of his work had been done on one-man operated vehicles. Jim kept and bred rabbits at the end of his garden and he thought he would be a rich man if he had a tanner for every time a passenger asked him how his rabbits (or did they say "rabbuhs") were?

On 26th September 1951 the village of Hyde End got its first service when the 394 was extended from Hyde Heath.

Instantly recognisable as Beaconsfield, this photograph taken on 7th October 1951 captures so much period charm. The old cars, road signs, family group and of course the bus, all form a nostalgic glimpse into our local history. The 1935 20-seater Leyland Cub, C37 is operating on the 398A route heading towards Amersham.
Photograph courtesy of A B Cross collection.

With just two years' service for LT left to do for C57, she had been new in July 1935 and spent most of her war years in red, white and brown livery working in the Central Area. Converted back to country green and white in 1949 and photographed at Amersham Garage on 10th February 1952 whilst operating on Route 353 (presumably during a slack period as she has only 20-seats).
Photograph courtesy of A B Cross collection.

Big fright for Driver Ferguson

In May 1952 John W C Ferguson from Hill Side, Chalfont St. Peter was driving an Amersham based double-decker on the Ley Hill to High Wycombe route. It was a hazy misty morning and they were on an open stretch of road, John had his side lights on. He saw a car coming towards him in the opposite direction and had no cause for concern until a lorry pulled out from behind him in an overtaking manoeuvre. Neither vehicle had any escape route and there was a terrible head-on collision. Thomas Wright aged 24, of Wey Lane, Chesham was a front upstairs passenger on the bus and he said the lorry came from nowhere. Philip Jones of Winchmore Hill, the lorry driver, tried in court to accuse the car driver of speeding but the judge wasn't in any mood to consider that defence, and fined him £2/11/0 for bad driving.

Further advertising from London Transport in May 1952 again saw a drive to promote local coach tours departing from The Chilterns. These now included trips to Hampton Court, return fare from Hemel Hempstead 6/-; to the Royal Tournament including admission, return fare 11/- and to the "London Transport private enclosure" for Ascot Gold Cup races 7/6.

Overcrowding was often an issue at busy times and in December 1952 the TGWU (Transport and General Workers Union), representing the busmen, declared in the local press that their members would strictly adhere to the policy of no standing on one-man operated vehicles and a maximum of five standing on all other vehicles during permitted hours. A very supportive letter was published the following week from a member of the public, who agreed their stance. He said that pressure needed to be brought in order that more services were put in place to cover increased demand.

An unusual photograph to appear in a book about the Amersham LT Country Bus Garage. It was taken on 5th July 1952, the last day of trams running in Lewisham. Judging by the way tramcar 1864 is at the centre of the photograph, it seems the photographer thought the inclusion of a brand-new RF coach was probably something of a distraction. Green Line MLL792 RF255 had only been delivered new the previous month and is out working on Route 703 with destination blind set for its run back to Amersham. The RF was set to become the single-deck workhorse for LT and ultimately replace the long running T-type vehicles.
Photograph courtesy M A Timms.

Years later Ernie Revel recalled that Britain was finally returning to normal although some things were still rationed. From February 1953 the children could again buy a few sweets; sherbet had just come into the shops. What greater joy than boarding your bus after school with a freshly bought sherbet fountain? Sucking gently through your straw of liquorice, the fizzing sherbet would dust the tongue; too hard and it hit the back of your throat causing an instant powder cloud to be blown like a blizzard towards fellow bus passengers, the child left coughing and eyes watering!

In May 1953 the old "sheds" (see page 15), that had formed the original garages for the Amersham & District Motor Bus Company since the early 1920s, were demolished. By this time a Mr J Burrows was renting them from London Transport and he wanted to place a much more modern private car sale and repair enterprise on the site. Those original wooden army huts and later corrugated iron buildings comprised about 400 square yards and had held approximately one dozen single-decker buses.

During 1953 the last three STL-types to be operated on Route 305 from Amersham were finally replaced by the new post-war RT-type. On 7th October after 19 years of absence, Chesham's Pond Park Estate once again benefitted from a bus service when the 348A started running through the estate via Hivings Hill, Upper Belmont Rd and Lyndhurst Rd. Christmas Day operations were slashed this year, with only the 353 and Green Line's 703 & 710 running.

A replacement for the pre-war Leyland Cubs came in the form of the 26-seat Guy Special (GS). London Transport ordered 84 for delivery in 1953. They were built to a London Transport specification for one-man operation on country lane routes that were sparsely trafficked. Interior ventilation was by small sliding windows at the top, gone were the days when you could wind or pull down the side windows for maximum air flow. Amersham received their first allocations that December. At this time the garage started working with about ten of the little buses operating on routes 348, 373, 397, 398. Its design harked back over two decades to vehicles like the 1930 Dennis GLs from the old A&D days; the GS even had a crash gearbox (i.e. no synchro-mesh) and therefore required a driving skill that was already being lost. They did, however, make a pretty sight nipping around the Chiltern countryside, pushing their "Indian Head" noses down verdant country lanes and shooing rabbits and squirrels in their path. With the launch of this vehicle, virtually all the final remnants of pre-war bus operations were dispensed with, excepting a few remaining T-types. Amersham would now operate pretty much unchanged with RT, RLH, RF and GS vehicles meeting all their needs for the next decade, the last GS left Amersham in October 1962. Many a small boy will fondly remember these very individual vehicles looking like something from Enid Blyton's "Noddy" books. I particularly recall they had a pruning saw mounted in the driver's cab. I always assumed it was for rapid removal of overhanging branches but was subsequently told it was for cutting through the wooden side bars between the road-wheels thus allowing anything trapped under the vehicle to be removed.

The GS radiator is capped by a glorious Red Indian's head with full headdress. The logo "FEATHERS IN OUR CAP" appeared in the 1920s in tandem with the advertising of some prestigious orders they had secured. The slogan was quickly followed by the adoption of a full Indian's head mascot.

This photograph dates to early 1954 and shows newly arrived GS62 taking on passengers for Route 398 to Beaconsfield. The new vehicle had been delivered to Amersham in December 1953 and moved to Garston in April 1954. It very briefly returned to MA in 1962. Notice how the radiator grille is split horizontally in half, this allows the bonnet to be lifted, at which time it gives the whole front the look of a wonderful green crocodile with gaping jaws.

Photograph courtesy of A B Cross collection.

A mark of respect

On Thursday 29th April 1954 Amersham LT garage closed its doors and the personnel stood in front of them as the funeral cortège of 39-year old Mrs Maureen Percival passed down the road. Maureen had been a conductress on the Green Line coaches; she had worked at the garage since the closing months of the war. Wreaths were sent from Supervisory and Clerical staff LTE, the LTE Amersham Sports & Social Club, LTE Incidental Fund and The Girls at Amersham Garage.

Staff shortages became a major problem for LT and it played havoc with timetables. Although Amersham had run one-man-operated (OMO) buses since the days of the old A&D it was now time to start running bigger vehicles as driver only. The first change in this era took place on 11th August 1954 and that was the running of RF-type vehicles out of Two Waters Garage in Hemel Hempstead on Route 316 to Chesham. The old-style Bell Punch tickets were now starting to be phased out, prices were rising and the ticket issuing system needed more flexibility. Initially "Ultimate" ticket machines were used on this route and the combination proved highly successful. However, "Gibson" ticket machines would soon follow and be adopted throughout the LT network. The continued staff shortages at Amersham resulted in Route 710 being temporarily withdrawn on 3rd October 1954, followed 10 days later by a cut back in operations on the 336. Route 359 (Amersham-Aylesbury) was handed over to Eastern National. Other cut-backs were made on 305/A, 353 and 362/A routes. The Board started another recruiting campaign, this time in Ireland; it proved successful with enough staff taken on to cover the immediate shortages. Full services were re-instated from 20th October 1954.

The fact that staff were in such short supply and overtime plentiful, didn't stop Amersham garage driver Victor Lloyd Dwight of 3 Hill Meadow, Coleshill, signing up, at Amersham Magistrate's Court, to become a Special Constable in December 1954. Vic as he was known always smoked a pipe while driving his bus and no passenger ever seems to have moaned about any blue haze he produced, however, drivers taking over from him certainly knew he'd been around! Vic was also a St. John Ambulance volunteer and a trained first aider. Wonderful community spirit from Vic.

Chapter 5   More Recruitment Problems (1955–1959)

A full London Transport Country Bus Services uniform from the mid-1950s, complete with Gibson roll fed ticket machine. This heavy serge uniform was initially worn winter and summer, the only difference in summer was the issue of a white cover to their caps, actually making them thicker than in winter!
Images courtesy of London Transport Museum collection.

Although understandably not appreciated by the Board at the time, passenger numbers would now start to fall; the peak had been reached and henceforth the private motor car would become king of the road in ever greater numbers. However, the bus fleet was now fairly well standardised and the predominant RT-type double-deckers and RF-type single-deckers would prove reliable vehicles that became loved by staff and passengers across the LT network.

Chesham magistrate says "Fitters should not drive buses alone".

In June 1955 Philip Charles Maxwell Hunt, a fitter for LTE at Amersham, reversed a 30-foot Green Line coach into a stationary car at the bottom of Nashleigh Hill, Chesham. Hunt of "Osterley" First Avenue, Amersham accepted that his mirrors and rear window had not allowed him to see the saloon car as it was too close behind him, he was fined £3/-/-. The magistrate suggested that in future LTE make sure their fitters are accompanied when out testing buses and coaches. Mr Hunt had intended to turn the vehicle around at the foot of Nashleigh Hill but could not complete the manoeuvre without reversing; the saloon car driver was unaware of his intentions and waited behind the bus only to get hit as it reversed. Mr Hunt had held a clean licence for 20 years.

Another far more serious accident happened just weeks later in Chesham.

This one sadly proved fatal for a motorcyclist at Red Lion Corner, Chesham. The aftermath scene appeared in the Bucks Examiner. A public outcry ensued calling for a change to a safer road layout. LLU686 is RT 3887 operating on Route 362 to Ley Hill.

Photograph published in The Bucks Examiner 9th September 1955, courtesy of The British Library.

Now for role reversal, as the bus becomes the ambulance.

It was cold, frosty and foggy on 30th November 1955, a bus on route 353 was travelling between Amersham and Chalfont St. Giles when the driver came across an accident involving a car and a lorry. The lady driving the car had a bad head injury and the bus crew stopped to offer assistance. An ambulance was most certainly needed but there was no phone box in the vicinity and her blood loss meant time was of the essence. Driver Borlase (age 25) and conductor Stearn (age 26), both from Windsor, took the instant decision to drive the patient to the Chalfonts and Gerrards Cross Hospital. Mrs B Newman of Chesham Bois made a full recovery and sent her grateful thanks to London Transport for the prompt action of their staff, she felt they saved her life and as a token of her appreciation she presented the driver and conductor with a cheque each for Christmas.

A friendly uniformed London Transport bus conductor, still using his Bell Punch rack of tickets, was even used in a 1955 G-Plan furniture advert. With High Wycombe being such a centre for the furniture industry, we can assume local conductors might offer such help, especially where an attractive young lady was concerned.

Bus Ride – Clive Birch

Clive Birch was a well-known local historian, writer and newspaper columnist and editor. This short story was published in the Bucks Examiner in 1956; it reads as though it might have been penned some years before that date.

"Lurching headlong through the soft darkness of the crude yielding of the country night, the bus ground round corners, howled up hills, clearing its throat as they got steeper and groaning in despair until the heights were reached; then a final heaving shudder, and it gasped along the cloud-flecked lanes.

Jangling and jumping like the face of nerve-ridden soldier, after a patrol in the spineless quiet of a war-night, the passengers pat-patted the stiff seat backs, as they swayed their bodies with the motion of the bus.

Near the front, under a fitful bulb, one of four that dimly lit the interior, sat the conductor, money-pouch swung across the scarce swathed bulging thighs, warped cap on the stack of roving hair. His was a wide sloping back, all unaware of the sweating, slavering bus.

The rivulets of condensation found their way down his spectacles, and irritated his grimed cheek. Impatiently, he rubbed the place, and the rasp of nails on his growth stirred the vacuum of quiet with the tearing noise of the bus, as it fought on up the hills and round the corners.

Suddenly, it gave a series of pants and grinding coughs; the windows shook almost out of their sockets as it came to a standstill. The conductor hoisted himself into the narrow central space, and dragged to the door, at the rear.

He peered mirthlessly through the murky window, and hauled on the sliding door, jerking it open. A child, socks draped round its ankles, short, too short, overcoat buttoned tight to its throat, dank hair across its eyes, stumbled up and into the seat opposite.

The door stuck. The conductor kicked at it. The door still held against him, and he kicked again. Almost, it seemed to cringe, and then, unexpectedly, apologetically perhaps, ran into place, shaking the whole bus. One or two passengers half-woke, and resettled themselves as the bus, after grating and heaving, gathered itself forward.

The conductor mumbling in his teeth, and scraping his hand across his cheek, approached the child staring up at him. Hand held out, the conductor swayed above him, asked for the fare. The child grubbed in a pocket, came forth empty-handed; rummaged in other pockets and grasped a miniature pouch in imitation leather. At that moment the bus lurched sideways and slithered and scratched against the hedge, as a pair of white beams whined by, and, in that moment, the purse slipped and vanished under a seat. The conductor turning back to the child, from watching the car pass, held his hand out again and the child shook its head. The conductor remonstrated, and waived his hand in front of the frightened staring eyes. The child said nothing, only pointed to its tortured lips, mouthing silent. Still, the conductor ranted, and, raised his hand up, brought it across the seat-back with a thud that jolted the child forward. The child shook its head, the sweat sparkling, like silver dust. Suddenly, the conductor shrugged and plunged a hand into his pocket, brought out a handful of greasy coppers, and selecting five, poured them into the money-pouch. He punched a ticket, gave it to the child, who held it away, wondering, and stared at the swaying back, as it lolled down the passage to the front seat.

The bus shed several passengers; all save one man, in a remote grey coat with woollen gloves, whose face was wreathed in smoke curls from a short, black pipe. The child vanished into the dark cavern of the door, the last to leave, save this one man.

As the bus ran into the village, where lights peered into the windows, the man leant forward to the floor, and picked up a dark object, the purse.

He smiled at the conductor and handed him the purse, before he disappeared.

The conductor followed him into the darkness.
The noise of the village was dulled in the lane outside the garage, as the bus rolled its length away into the depths of the shed and glowed red in the reflection of the rear light. The conductor took off his glasses, blew hoarsely at them, and rubbed them on his sleeve. Then he looked closely at the purse and saw the two scraps of paper, tucked in the flap. One was a pound note, the other a page torn from a book. It was creased and soiled but two lines stood against the greyness of the rest; two lines confronted him, ringed in pencil. "Suffer the little children to come unto Me, and, forbid them not, for of such is The Kingdom of God".
(The above story has been re-printed with the kind permission of Clive Birch, a lifelong lover of all things Chesham and Amersham.)

This photograph of Amersham conductress Rita Reece was taken around 1956 when she was operating on the 394A route. The vehicle is T783 and is one of the last T-types operated by LT. This bus ended up being sold to Ceylon in 1958.
Photograph courtesy of Amersham Museum.

Country Bus Rover tickets will be well remembered by many from the older generation; a one-day freedom pass to go where you liked on LT's green bus fleet. A day spent travelling to all the places that excited you most, eating on the go so as not to waste a precious second of the time available. Bus map in hand and always an eye on your watch. These joyous passes became available from 1st July 1956 at five shillings per day. They were supposed to only be issued in the summer months to September but proved such a big hit they continued until further notice. (By November that year London Transport had sold 127,000 Rover tickets).

A letter to the Bucks Examiner in August gave a suggested afternoon trip from Chesham, all for just a 5/- Rover ticket *"In spite of the storms and rain our outings so far have been carried out in fine weather – here is a half-day trip in the dry after a wet morning which promised a hopeless day and then relented; Chesham to Wycombe (1:38 Broadway); alight at the bus stop going downhill into Wycombe, walk down to the main road and turn left for Staines bus (which passes through Farnham and Slough with countryside on route to Windsor); at Staines, tea at Dexter's (in main road); a river visit and then to Windsor for an hour or two with the setting sun lighting up the river; from Windsor home, a beautiful evening run".* Sounds idyllic even today, let alone 1956.

Will Randall who was the original General Manger of the Amersham & District Motor Bus Co. passed away on 5th August 1956. He had become District Superintendent of the Western District of the Country Bus and Coach section for London Transport. This was formed out of the old A&D area of operation with their Amersham offices designated as the new District Office. He had retired in 1947 on grounds of ill health, aged just 55. Will had been on sick leave from LT since December 1945; he had spent all 28 years of his service in the Amersham district. His health deteriorated with diabetes and blindness, his granddaughter remembers reading the newspapers to him in the 1950s and helping him with his horse racing selections; a pastime not exactly approved of by his wife. Will passed away having not yet reached the official retirement age of 65. In a notice in the local press, Will's family thanked their GP Doctor Starkey and staff at Amersham Hospital for their kindness. Will Randall is buried in Penn cemetery.

Bus services were now set to be hit by petrol rationing again. Towards the end of 1956 the Suez Crisis flared up, causing fuel shortages. Emergency service timetables were introduced on 17th December, although Green Line routes were left unaffected. However, the shortages also hit the private motorist and they had no alternative but to turn back to public transport. So, bus and coach demand rose during the crisis which lasted until the end of March 1957.

Lifelong resident of Ley Hill, Margaret Long remembered that "well into the 1950s great queues would develop at the end of summer Sunday afternoons as visitors began waiting outside The Crown public house for the buses to take them home". But the great expansion of private car ownership had already started and, although slowed by the Suez Crisis, was seemingly unstoppable. As traffic increased the local authorities started to put in more measures for road safety. A black spot for mainly minor accidents was Amersham's Oakfield Corner junction and in January 1957 traffic lights were installed to control movement.

Death at Ballinger involving a London Transport bus.

At 10:30 pm on 17th February 1957 Reginald Albert Richardson (aged 51) was driving his London Transport bus in Ballinger when it was involved in a collision with a car driven by Gordon Whitney. Sadly, the crash was such that Mr Whitney's mother Eileen sustained serious injuries, she died at Amersham Hospital some days later. Mrs Whitney came from Handcross, South Heath. Driver Richardson lived at 20 Vale Rise, Chesham.

Strike at Amersham Garage.

Towards the end of July, Amersham drivers on the Amersham Station to Aylesbury route refused to drive their buses beyond Great Missenden. This action was taken to support United Counties drivers who also drove the section and were involved in the national busmen's strike. It was the only route affected from Amersham garage.

German Storm-troopers capture London Road, Amersham!

That same month, bus crews would have been aghast to be stopped by lorry loads of jack-booted Germans controlling the entire London Road in the area of Mantells Farm. The Waffen SS were about to capture the farmstead as part of a Pinewood Studios film called "Carve her name with pride". Starring Jack Warner and Virginia McKenna, it was the story of heroic British SOE undercover agent Violette Szabo and her eventual capture at a French farm in WW2. The Nazis executed Violette in February 1945, she was 23. Britain awarded her the George Cross.

We surely must consider a collective noun for a group of Guys like this. How about a brotherhood? Photograph taken in one of the old A&D garages that were still in use by LT at this time.
Photograph courtesy of Amersham Museum.

In the late 1950s all older buses on LT's fleet had flashing indicators fitted, they were operated by a large palm sized red knob in the driver's cab. Hand signals had been the main order of the day for most bus drivers until now.

The deeply sad news of driver Frederick Macdonnell

Frederick loved being one of Amersham garage's bus drivers. In fact, it is true to say he lived for the job. In October 1957, after many years in the role, he started to suffer some mental health issues and was relieved of driving duties. He left the company to work as an aerial erector. He deeply missed his former role and LT offered him a job as a conductor. However, Frederick felt he was of little use anymore and sadly took his own life. His job driving Amersham buses had meant so much to him. Frederick lived in the pre-fabs on White Lion Road, Amersham.

The year of 1958 will be remembered for a much longer and more disastrous six-week bus strike that started in May. It was an action from the busmen that did not do well and resulted in a loss of passenger traffic amounting to nearly twenty percent. Although Amersham's engineers were not on strike they supported the operating staff by "downing tolls", instead playing cards and dominos in the canteen for the duration. Passengers resorted to all sorts of methods to travel and parents rallied round to sort out their school children. The most unusual solution being the bunch of 30 kids who travelled daily from Winchmore Hill to Penn Street in the back of an open lorry. By all accounts they loved it! Posh children from the Chalfonts had a private bus hired for them at a cost of £4/5/0 a day. Union strike pay was all but impossible to live on and a number of LT staff left after a few weeks. Among them was Wilf Brackley who started a new job but decided to return to LT once things were back to normal. Wilf had become very disillusioned as workmates started to fall out during the dispute. Cleaners and engineers were put on the spot when the strike ended suddenly and the languishing Amersham fleet now had flat batteries, flat tyres and the cobwebs of inactivity to be speedily remedied.

Ex-STL1470 CXX457 converted to tree lopping duties and given service vehicle number 971J, seen here in preservation. On the right could this shadowy visitor to the forecourt of the Amersham garage be 971J? Left photograph N Lamond; Right photograph from unknown source but thank you for taking an appropriate snap for this page.

Country bus routes regularly needed to be cleared of overhanging branches and this duty fell upon London Transport's tree pruning service. It was not unusual to see one of the above type vehicles tucked away at Amersham garage. These open toppers were retired double-deck buses, generally from the country fleet, they were specifically modified for this role. The one in the main photograph has survived into preservation and generally operated out of St. Albans or Garston garages but served Amersham's needs when required. This 1936 vehicle retired from passenger duties after 17 years, including wartime service, and continued as this useful service vehicle until late 1963 when it was sold to become a caravan.

Conductor Norman Freeman's "Brief Encounter" with 1950s skirts

Norman's own account of this event "*I was working one day on the 336 with my driver Lionel Humphrey, it would have been about 1958. We arrived at Chenies on our way to Watford; waiting at the stop were three very attractive girls, dressed to the nines in the latest fashion skirts. I am sure you can picture them, large circle skirts with reams of nylon petticoats that made them open out like lampshades. The girls turned out to be from Holland and wanted to go to Watford. My bus was a double-decker with an open platform; they possibly wanted to smoke as they all went upstairs. I dutifully followed to collect their fares, it seems I was a little too quick, as the last one to board was still only half-way up when a gust of wind caught her skirt and enveloped me in the billowing canopy. All went dark, I never wore a hat, was often in trouble for not doing so, but that day it might have been a blessing. I won't say I emerged*

Sketch drawn by Danny Champion and Neil Lamond.

looking like Captain Mainwaring but I can tell you, I've remembered it all my life and pleased to report that the girl was most concerned". (Author's note: a Bucks Examiner article from August 1958 contains a report about a group of Dutch tourists who visited Amersham from their home town of Amersfoort. These visits became regular occurrences as the towns were twinned).

Not every report that you uncover in research is pleasant to recall. In December 1958, a Green Line crew operating on Route 703 found themselves in court on a charge of theft. Driver Herbert Wood (29) and conductor Eric Revitt (43) where accused of stealing a handbag with a value of £32/6/6. The bag had been accidentally left on their coach and it seems was subsequently stolen by this Amersham based crew. They pleaded guilty; Wood got three years' probation and Revitt two years.

Here we see Green Line RF20 registration no. LUC220 in London's Regent Street on a bright April day in 1959. This vehicle was originally introduced as a private hire coach in 1951 and has attractive glazed cant roof panels, it is also fitted with luggage racks. It is operating on Amersham's Route 709 Chesham – London – Caterham. Some of these newly built private hire RFs had been used carrying visitors to The Festival of Britain. LUC220 was sold in 1963 when London Transport staff shortages forced them to withdraw from the private hire market, this vehicle survives in preservation.
Photograph courtesy of A B Cross collection.

Another tale from around this time concerns an Amersham driver called Taffy Griffiths. Taffy was driving an RF-type down the hill from Wigginton to Tring, suddenly he felt the vehicle hesitate and come to halt. Taffy revved the engine hard, but to no avail. He got out to see if it was anything obvious and found his bus had sunken into the tarmac road surface. By the time the recovery lorry arrived, the RF's bodywork was touching the road. With the aid of some planks, the vehicle was pulled clear with no resultant damage. The road was closed off for some while and this section was later by-passed by the Council workmen. Taffy went on to become an Inspector.

The old Wigginton finger post sign

81

Now it only requires a small amount imagination to join the above two photographs together to provide a clear panoramic picture of how the old and new Amersham garages looked on 29th August 1959. It was very far sighted of Mr Gillham to capture both images.

Photographs taken by J C Gillham, courtesy of A B Cross.

Christmas Parties on the Green Line

Travelling to London together on the Green Line day after day allowed new friendships to emerge. At Christmas it was not unusual for parties to be planned for the last journeys back before the festive break. Customers would gather and celebrate at the back of the coach. Norman Freeman remembers them well and even being passed the odd bottle of booze as a Christmas box when passengers disembarked. Receiving tips at Christmas from regular customers was commonplace at this period, especially if you were a well-known driver or conductor. Norman remembers the crews on T-type vehicles on Route 394 to Tring, received particularly generous tips every December (T-type buses ceased to run at Amersham during 1958, however, one remained in service stationed at Tring until late 1962).

Chapter 6   The Motor Car Moves Ahead (1960-1969)

This decade heralded changes that would significantly alter bus usage and bring about a wholesale rethink for public motor passenger transport. Private car ownership had been dramatically increasing throughout the 1950s and during this coming decade most 17-year olds would aspire to own their own car as soon as they could pass their driving test. The car offered convenience, practicality, warmth and status. Households with televisions now approached 100% and queues for the bus home after the cinema finished were diminishing. In fact, the Regent Cinema in Amersham closed in 1962. Change on this scale would continue to affect public transport requirements for years to come. More change would come in the 1980s as more and more of our precious youth started to be cosseted in private cars to and from school, the humble bus services had a lot more suffering to endure.

A wonderful result for Amersham Garage came with the presentation of the "1960 Safe Driver Awards" for both bus and coach drivers. For the year the following were honoured:-
27-year Bronze Bar: F G Woodman. 21-24 year Star Bars: W J (Jim) Chapman (24), L J Harris (23), F Redding (23), A W Harrowell (22), Tom F Stickland (22), A Brown (21), A A Hopkins (21), George L Stokes (21). 20-year Brooches: Albert Parrott, S A Stubbs, H Phelby. 16-19 year Bars: E I Old (19), A F (Frank) Shrimpton (19), Alf C Smith (19), J H Wright (19), A Bolton (18), C W Crumpler (18), A J Gray (18), T Hoare (18), K J Burge (18), W Hance (17), H C Estlin (16), M E Lacey (16), K R Strickland (16). 15-year Brooch: R (Dick) G Bastin. 11-14 year Oak Leaf Bars: L C Bryant (14), J (Bing) Crosby (14), J H Redrup (14), Wilf E Saint (14), C Sharpe (14), C W Keen (13), Ernie J Revel (13), W J (John) Holdcroft (12), S W Shaw (12), Harold G Cleaton (11), R F Elms (11), W J Ferguson (11), F C James (11). 10-year Medals: Ernie A Bishop, Don H Pearce, E J (Jack) Whitebread. 6-9 year Bars: Ron A Baldwin, J H Catling, S Freeman, A (Taffy) Griffiths, L W Humphrey, Peter J Jeeves, W J Johnson, J Matthews, Arthur B Reed, A S (Sid) Rogers, Frank W Walker. 5-year Medals: L F Arnold, A E Weller, S H Wyatt.

GREEN LINE POSTER DATED 1960 and showing the typical style of the period. According to the Bucks Examiner a handful of Green Line coaches were the only passenger vehicles that ran from our area on Christmas day 1960.
Image copyright courtesy of TfL from the London Transport Museum collection.

Amersham Green Line coach given Police escort round Buckingham Palace

A true story from circa 1961 when Bert Brown (driver) and Norman Freeman (conductor) operated as a crew. This time they were working on the Green Line service 710 to Crawley. *"It was a normal day taking our usual passengers down to Victoria and then travelling on to Crawley. We got into London with ease; there wasn't much traffic in those days. We encountered an inspector who told us of road closures and we now needed to go down this road and turn right up that road etc. Well we were sure this wasn't right as we ended up driving down The Mall and onto the roundabout in front of Buckingham Palace. A pincer movement of police cars brought us to a halt for questioning!* "What do you think you are doing? Buses aren't allowed down here", "Sorry but our inspector told us to come this way", "Well he is ****** wrong".

The police did no more than put one squad car in front of us and one behind and gave us a personal escort round the roundabout and all the way off to Victoria. We had to file a detour report when we got back to Amersham and tell them about our encounter with the long arm of the law. The inspector got the sack. For years this was considered the only crew bus ever on service to go around Buckingham Palace and it became known as the "Brown and Freeman detour". Good fun for a 6/- single fare to London on the 710.

Amersham based RF238 operating GREEN LINE Route 703. This photograph was probably taken in the late 1950s or early 1960s.
Photographer unknown, John Hutchinson collection.

Two interior photographs from a Green Line RF coach now in preservation at the London Bus Museum. Note the overhead luggage racks.

In January 1961, Green Line offered special family trips inclusive of entrance tickets to see either the circus at Olympia or the Wembley Ice Show. Tickets could be bought at the Garage and passengers picked up at various points along the way. They proved popular as they were pretty much a door to door service and, if on the return leg, passengers needed an onward local bus that had stopped running, then Green Line undertook to drop them nearer to their own home. They repeated the offer again in 1962 with various price levels up to 15/6 for adults and 11/6 for children. Although in this case the Green Line offering beat the train, by September 1961 the railway between Rickmansworth and Amersham was electrified. New train services were soon introduced to benefit from this and all took their toll on bus passenger numbers, especially on Green Line Route 703. Also, by 1961 the Sunday bus traffic on the 336 had fallen such that the Sunday service was withdrawn from 22nd October.

Arthur Gurney, aged 61, a London Transport bus driver for 28 years, sadly had his 45-year unblemished driving licence history marred following an accident on the Berkhampstead Road in September 1961. Arthur was driving back into Chesham from Tring when he had to pass a stationary van on his side of the road. He felt there was enough room to pass both the van and an oncoming refuse lorry; however, the two collided at very low speed in the manoeuvre. To Arthur's utmost displeasure the police prosecuted him and he had his licenced endorsed and was fined £5/0/0 with 5/- costs. Arthur was so infuriated he appealed, again lost, and this time incurred a further £20 fine for costs.

This story came in from Geoff Campbell, following a request for information about the Amersham LT garage, *"I phoned my cousin who lived in Amersham in the 1960s. He worked for a time at the Brazils factory and recalls that one night in the early 1960s there was an explosion at the factory which resulted in damage to the bus garage roof. It occurred because there was a rotating drum used for processing offal which was fuelled by benzene. The machine was known by Brazil's staff as the bomb. Someone omitted to replace the top of the fuel tank after filling it up and the resultant vapour was ignited by the pilot light of a heater in the bays where the lorries were stored and loaded. The explosion wrecked the roof of the factory; the railway that fed the machine also caused damage to the bus garage roof. Several of the Company's lorries were also damaged or destroyed".*

Here we see GS65 picking up passengers in Chesham on 20th May 1961. The little antennae sprouting from the top of the nearside front wing had a small red ball on it and the drivers could use it to judge distances to the side of their vehicle. Little boy's fingers often gave them a tug (as John Hutchinson remembers only too well).
Photograph courtesy of Photofive Transport Enterprises.

A nice 1960's photograph of RLH44 working Route 336. In a later chapter you will see exactly what happened to this very bus.
Photograph John Hutchinson collection.

A photograph included to bring a smile to your face. This RT is seen at the back of High Wycombe garage and it is thought that rolling the blind out of the back window was just done as a prank for the camera. Certainly, an activity that could have brought trouble to the pranksters, who just might have been put up to it by Mark Adlington! The text on the blind in capital letters indicates and early 1960s picture.
Photograph courtesy of Amersham Museum.

A Gibson machine bounces off a 336

Yet another of Norman Freeman's stories, *"One day around 1962, Bert Brown was my driver at the time, we were together for 5 years from 1961, a great partnership. Bert had been on the buses for years and went right back to the old Amersham & District days, everyone knew Bert. We were running a 336 up to Oakfield Corner, top Amersham, and Bert spotted that he could turn right without stopping as there was nothing around; my trouble was I hadn't got my Gibson ticket machine strapped on at that point and I was thrown off balance at the rear of the lower deck. In a split second the Gibson was gone from my grasp, took one bounce on the platform, then off the back of the bus, jumping frog like onto Sycamore Road with an injuring clatter. The wall of Barclays Bank took the full brunt of the impact. I got Bert to stop and went to retrieve what remained, there was no hope it would work again so I placed it back in the box in which it had been issued to me that day. I now had to revert to the old Bell Punch tickets. Although I started as a conductor in 1954, I was the first one at Amersham, trained on using the new roll fed machines and had never touched the old pre-printed tickets at all. It was a new experience for me, better than the one I suffered when I got back at the end of my shift. Like all cheeky chaps I thought, I'll hand in my Gibson in its box and hope they don't notice – wrong, the damage was spotted immediately and I had to own up. I was given something of a telling off, I can tell you, extending to threats that I would have to pay for it".*

A typical Amersham sight in the early 1960's, RLH 48 working Route 336 to Watford and waiting to take on passengers, the summer uniformed (light "dust" jackets became an option around this time) conductor chatting away merrily to a colleague. The scene being recreated here at a vintage bus running day in Amersham.
Photograph N Lamond.

A rare night time photograph inside an RT with the brown concertina blinds closed and masking reflected light into the driver's cabin. The Amersham crew captured here are Driver John Bartall and Conductress Mary Wells (we see Mary again later in this book). Mark Adlington probably took the photograph when this crew returned to the depot one evening.
Photograph courtesy of Amersham Museum.

The last of the very cute GS buses ran from Amersham on 23rd October 1962, RFs took over their duties the following day. The Garage had eleven of Guy Specials at this stage although only nine were needed for normal daily operations and two were spares. Some were transferred to Garston and they continued in service until March 1972, running out to Rickmansworth and Loudwater. For the first time in 26 years, on 28th October 1962 the Sunday service of the 316 was operated by one-man buses provided by Amersham running to Ley Hill from Amersham Garage. This was in place of the weekday 362/A services.

Sport had played a vital part in the off-duty lives of garage staff since the original founding days of the Sports and Social Club back in A&D's time. The next photograph must be sometime after 1961 as that was the year that Wally Lally moved to Amersham from Alperton. The Club would also arrange outings; Albert Palser's children remember trips to the coast in the 1950s and a visit or two to the Amersham Theatre (now an auction room on Station Road). Albert worked at the garage in administration and was "Charge Depot Inspector" for a short time.

The Amersham Garage football team from the 1960s. L-R Back Row: not recorded, not recorded, Brian Valder, Norman Freeman, Wally Lally, not recorded; Front Row: not recorded, Jock Spence, Taffy Griffiths, Billy Gahan, not recorded.

The Prettiest Route on London Transport's Country Network

During the summer of 1963, London Transport staff were asked to submit nominations for, what was in their opinion, the prettiest route on which to travel. From the 300 or so country green bus routes many submissions favoured runs around Woking and Guildford, others included the 386 Bishop's Stortford to Hitchin. However, Amersham's 353 route was chosen by the editorial team to feature in a three-page article printed in the staff magazine that September.

Claimed to be the only route on the network that started and finished at an ancient castle (although Berkhamsted castle is no match for the grandeur of Windsor), the 353 also benefited from travelling its 25-mile length through numerous beauty spots, pretty villages and towns.

Following a stroll along the Thames you can board a 353 set for Berkhamsted, crossing over the river you move passed the famous old Eton School, possibly spotting a future Prime Minister as you go. Skirting the edge of Slough, you are now on a tree-lined lane screening barley fields behind. On approaching Stoke Poges, conductor Hugh Davies suggested many tourists get off here to see the place that inspired Thomas Gray to pen his "Elegy written in a country churchyard" arguably the most famous poem in the English language. The 18th century poet is buried in the village. The bus moves on to Gerrards Cross, the countryside ablaze with Rhododendrons in late April and May.

An RT leaving Chalfont St. Peter and passing the old horse drawn wagon.
This photographed accompanied the Staff Magazine article but is not credited to anyone.

The beautiful villages of the Chalfonts now beckon, first is St. Peter where an old horse drawn coach languishes by a country pub. Then on to St. Giles and "Milton's Cottage", where Paradise Lost was written, it is a must see for any traveller interested in literature.

A few miles down the Amersham Road with wonderful countryside views to your left and the Chiltern Hills to your right you enter the old market town of Amersham. A wooden sign dated 24th June 1811, affixed to the wall of an old cottage on the left, warns off beggars, ballad singers and other vagrants. The town is a feast for anyone's eyes; 400-year-old coaching inns jostle for position with an array of domestic architectural delights. The Old Town Hall stands sentinel as the bus squeezes by, the road opens out and offers a wide vista that screams out for the market stalls and charter fairs of days now gone. Passengers get a chance to see the street from both directions as the route caters to drop off people at the west end of town before it returns to make its way to new Amersham and then down a tree-lined hill on to Chesham.

The RT running on Route 353 passes The Kings Arms at Old Amersham
This photographed accompanied the Staff Magazine article but is not credited to anyone.

We move through Chesham, a town on the River Chess with a busy and packed, very narrow main street and make our way to Ashley Green. This stands out as yet another unspoilt hamlet before our journeys end at Berkhamsted. Now the possibility of a wander along the canal towpath, a look around the castle ruins and then a refreshing cuppa in a tea-shop. Could this route be beaten? I suspect you have to read all the staff magazines to find out. (The account originally published has been trimmed and re-written for this book but carries the same essential message. I am grateful to staff at the London Transport Museum for letting me use these snippets from their 1963 magazine. By now, new buildings, huge changes in traffic flow and parked cars will have altered one's views considerably, but it is still essentially a very pretty route on which to travel by bus). Despite this glowing testimonial for the 353, on 10th May 1964 a summer experiment started on Route 353 when alternate Sunday buses were an express service to Windsor, only stopping at 15 points on the journey. This could have stopped people disembarking to enjoy some of the beauty spots along the way. The experiment was not repeated the following year. Later in 1964 Green Line Route 703 finally succumbed to falling passenger numbers and was withdrawn on 3rd November.

A photograph that will be a familiar scene for many and taken around the mid-1960s. The lovely original hanging lamps are still in place above every entrance. The road works screened off by wooden barriers and oil warning lamps.

Photographer details not known but acknowledged by us for its lovely period feel, thank you.

Left: **Rita Reece in full LT conductor's uniform of the mid-1960s.**

As we head into 1965 there is a general undercurrent of dissatisfaction with many of the local bus services which seem to have been cut back beyond reason. In February a delegation of local authorities pressed for a Ministerial Review into country bus services, such was their concern. London Transport was watching intently, but their passenger traffic was falling and they needed to make cuts; things could not remain the same. Green Line came out fighting and slashed off-peak prices after Easter. Travelling into London with the new "Cheap Day Return" would cost one third less, Chesham to Oxford Street return now 8/6 a saving of 4/10.

Chesham June 1965, RF 307 (NLE526) with smashed nearside front windscreen awaits recovery from the old London Transport "Breakdown Tender" parked behind it. Pupils from Lowndes School mill around inspecting the aftermath of this fatal incident. This 1953 RF-type started life as a coach designated RF 526. It became RF307 in 1956 and was converted for bus duties in 1962. Although it spent some time off the road after this accident, it went on to work from Amersham until May 1975 by which time it was 22 years old.

The photograph above appeared in the Bucks Examiner on 18th June 1965, courtesy of The British Library.

The tragic accident shown above occurred early on Saturday 12th June 1965. An RF-type (NLE526) heading for Chesham Broadway on Route 394, had come down Chartridge Lane and into the lower reaches of the road where it changes its name to Park Road (Lowndes Park being on the left as viewed in this photo). The bus has skidded out of control on a very wet surface and mounted the grass bank, in doing so inflicting fatal injuries to a pedestrian, Mr Henry Biffin aged 74. At the Coroner's inquest held at Chesham Police Station on 16th July, LT driver Harold Gilbert Cleaton, with 19 years bus driving experience, said his vehicle went into an uncontrollable skid whilst passing a parked mini-van on this very narrow road. He was only driving slowly at the time; this statement was verified by an off-duty policeman who was driving up the road and waiting for the bus to clear the obstruction. The bus hit Mr Biffin as he was walking on the footpath down the hill, it also impacted with a telegraph pole and lamp post. The Coroner recorded a verdict of "Misadventure". (Note: when Harold Cleaton eventually retired from LT he did periodic coach driving for Mr Ivins "The Pride of Bucks" fleet – see Chapter 8).

Passenger numbers were still falling year on year. In October it was announced that on London's country services they had recorded an annual fall of 4%. For weekends the picture was even bleaker, with an 8% fall on Saturdays and a massive 16% fall on Sundays. People were clearly using their private cars more at the weekends. At this stage the 316 route had been chopped down to a shuttle service from Ley Hill to Amersham, however even these special Sunday services to Ley Hill were withdrawn from 3rd October 1965. Many other local routes suffered cuts amounting to a 3% reduction in services and Route 336 saw the withdrawal of double-deck (RLH-type) operations in favour of one-man single deck vehicles. On 1st November 1965 the express operation of Route 709 was withdrawn but the 710 extended to Chesham to cover it. Additional coaches were also employed.

Here is RF694 operating on route 316 on a Sunday service in August 1965. During the week Route 316 skirted Ley Hill by running from Hemel Hempstead via Bovingdon Green, Orchard Leigh and down into Chesham, the weekday route had been operated by Rover Bus Services since 6th May 1964.

Photograph courtesy of James Whiting, Capital Transport; photographer unknown.

This photo of Ley Hill Common taken on a Bank Holiday around 1965 shows exactly how many came out to visit the village on a regular basis in those days. Ten years earlier and most of these people would have come by bus.

Photo courtesy Richard Sanders.

This RLH gets a wash and bows out from Amersham soon after. 1952 built RLH 35 MXX235 has been running on the 336 route to Watford, by October 1965 they were all retired from the garage. RLH 35 was at Amersham during late 1964 and into 1965 although it went on elsewhere to do another 5-years' service, it completed 18 years with London Transport before being sold on. It is still believed to be in preservation in Switzerland.

Photograph taken by David Bosher whom we know has died, if anyone else holds copyright we were unable to trace you.

February 1966 and RT998 is running on Route 362A destined for Ley Hill. The new style of destination blind featuring via points in lower case was supposed to make it easier to read. The advertisement on the side is for Sterling cigarettes at 4/7 for a packet of 20. Smoking was allowed on the top deck only but if you were on a single-deck vehicle it was supposedly restricted to the rear seats, in practice so many people smoked in those days that you certainly couldn't guarantee to be in smoke free zone anywhere on a single-decker.

Photograph taken by David Bosher whom we know has died, if anyone else holds copyright we were unable to trace you.

Driver Bill Perren a soft touch where animals are concerned

Bill was on the last shift driving his bus back to the garage when a baby rabbit froze in his headlights, it seemed unable to move. Whatever Bill did, the rabbit appeared glued to the tarmac, so he got down from the cab and was able to pick the little chap up. This appeared to be a wild rabbit that had lost its mum. With three daughters at home he knew they would love to look after it, so he took him up in the cab and brought him back, much to their delight. The little rabbit grew well and lived a number of years with the Perren family. If that wasn't enough a few years later Bill came home with a tiny kitten, the girls named it "Kitty" and fed it with a syringe for many weeks. "Kitty" became another household favourite and lived to the ripe old age of 16. Ahh Bill, you big softie.

The rather unusual positioning of this bus stop meant that the RT on Route 362 had to reverse around the corner on the right in order to park alongside it. The photograph is taken in the mid 1960's and is of the entrance to Kiln Lane at Ley Hill, a turnaround point for the 362 vehicles. The driver is Tom Stickland.
Photograph courtesy of Amersham Museum.

Driver Mark Adlington was a grammar school boy who just wanted to drive buses. During his career he took lots of photographs and after his death they were donated to Amersham Museum, some of them feature in this book. Mark also made the model of the bus garage that they usually have on display. Here we see Mark in RT 3259 (1966 or 67).
Photograph courtesy of Amersham Museum.

The miniskirt and boots would indicate a date around 1969/70. RT4117 operating from Amersham on the 362 has, for some reason, a very peculiar main blind that probably came from the side destination box as it was certainly never LTs intention to have the "362" repeated at the front.
Photograph courtesy of Amersham Museum.

London's most popular double-deck vehicle from this period was the ubiquitous Routemaster, however, Amersham was one of only two country garages to which they were never allocated. That does not mean they wouldn't be seen on the roads of Amersham and Chesham; other garages that shared the operation for longer routes would, from time to time, send in their Routemasters, it is therefore possible to come across photographs of them operating on the 353 for example.

A handful of new 36-feet long, one-man operated, AEC Merlin MB-type buses were allocated to Amersham in late 1968. The first two arrived as trial replacements for those venerable RTs still in operation. The Merlins were large single-deckers seating 45 people (25 in the raised rear section and 20 in the front). The drive to cut overheads had continued relentlessly, and on 23rd November 1968 Routes 305, 305A and 455 were converted to one-man operation. Very few routes now had conductors and the total demise of that role was just around the corner. Green Line operations on Route 710 between Amersham and Chesham now ceased, bringing an end to direct coach travel between Chesham and London that had started with A&D in January 1931. The Merlins set about operating on Route 305(A) and 455, but as neither of those routes passed the garage they could be used on 353 and 362(A) when returning "home". However, the vehicles were found to lack the manoeuvrability of the RTs and consequently only lasted a short while. Within a few weeks of their introduction as "driver-only" vehicles, LT started receiving complaints from peak hour passengers on the 305 route who were waiting up to 20 minutes longer and missing train connections at Gerrards Cross and Uxbridge.

The Swinging Sixties "Parties in a bus shelter" – Rates reduced.

Such was the newspaper headline that referred to a Rates appeal by Mr Erridge of Berkhampstead Road, Chesham. He complained that "juvenile parties with transistor radios" were taking place in the bus shelter that was partly in his front garden. In fact, the shelter took up 54% of his frontage, cut 5 feet into his garden and was only 25 feet from the house. He campaigned for a rate reduction; at a tribunal, the Council's Valuation Office said he didn't feel it warranted a discount; however, the Panel sided with Mr Erridge and awarded him a reduction in rateable value.

Wages still seem relatively low at this time, Ron Bovingdon (Jnr.) had joined at the end of 1968 and was paid £16/10/- per week for driving RTs. Fares rose substantially in 1969 as the company prepared to hand over control to the Greater London Council who wanted the country area operation placed on a more viable footing and needed to raise an additional £700,000 per annum.

During Easter 1969 Steve Fennell recalls having a conducted tour of Amersham Garage and observed "*A sea of green RTs and RFs awaited us and tucked away in the corner were two RTW training buses. The RTWs were being phased out from training duties by this time, so it was very much a surprise to see them there*". (Steve Fennell is now a transport author and running day organiser for the Amersham and District Motor Bus Society)

It seems amazing that right up until June 19th 1969 London Transport's Amersham bus garage still operated using the old 1920s A&D telephone number of "Amersham 36". Following what was described in the local press as being like "an American space-launch" the exchange moved to "Subscriber Trunk Dialling" precisely at 1:00 pm that day and the number became Amersham 4636. (Gosh, the Americans go to the moon in 1969 and we advance from 1920s telephone exchange numbers).

This photograph of "roof box" RT3496 (LYR915) and seemingly set to operate on Route 362, displaying nice period advertisements for BRANDON & SON of Chesham and GREEN ROVER tickets at 7/- each. This vehicle started its working life at Amersham in April 1952, it is now preserved in this most beautiful condition that emulates how they came back from overhauls at LT's Aldenham Works in the post-war period. In February 1969 Jeffrey Beard claimed he had hit the back of a bus in Red Lion Street, Chesham, because it was too shiny! He told Chesham magistrates he "must have been momentarily blinded by the glare". Fine £15 and licenced endorsed.
Photograph John Hutchinson collection.

Jim Chapman retires after 44 years......

Jim Chapman (left) had started out driving the 1922 Oldsmobile 14-seater and ended with the 1968 AEC Merlin shown below.

In his monumental career Jim Chapman began driving for the old Amersham & District Bus Co. in 1925 (see above photo). Almost unbelievably his professional working life spanned between operating hundreds of vehicles that plied the Amersham and Chesham roads up to 1969. One of the last vehicles he was to drive was AEC Merlin MB94 on the 353 route. The Merlins were 20% longer than the RFs. The photo above was taken a few months after he retired.
Photograph (left) Chapman family collection (right) John Hutchinson collection.

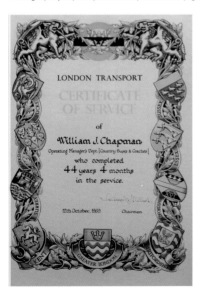

October 1969 Jim Chapman retired:

Jim Chapman had turned 65 the previous year but still enjoyed driving and decided he would carry on a little longer. However, early in 1969 and following a snowfall, he skidded whilst driving an AEC Merlin bus down through Chalfont St. Peter. He clipped a shop awning. Whilst this wasn't the only reason, it did contribute to him deciding to retire later that year. He felt he had seen the best years of bus driving. It had taken him from the 1920s when some children still walked barefoot to school, to the new era where almost everyone owned a car. Even after he left London Transport he still took on some odd delivery duties for a local business. He enjoyed his garden and remained friends with George Stokes who had also worked at the Garage. Jim did not enjoy a long retirement and he died in 1974.

Manoeuvrability wasn't the Merlins only problem. The existing bus stop bays had the concrete bus stop post sited towards the rear of the bay to facilitate the old rear entrance RT-type double-deckers taking on passengers. When a new Merlin entered the bay, the passengers moved forward to board at the front entrance; however, as the driver went to pull out from the bay the long (ten foot) overhang behind his rear wheels would swing leftwards and, in some cases, could strike the old bus stop.

The new and the old together. In the foreground we have the old stalwarts of an RT and an RF but behind them the rear of a new Merlin. The RF livery featuring the wide band beneath the windows started to appear in 1968.
Photograph courtesy of Amersham Museum.

On 15th February 1969 Route 353 vehicles from Amersham were converted to one-man operation using another new vehicle, the SM-type. Union trouble erupted in July with an overtime ban that started to hit operations badly. Despite the Union having agreed, in 1966, to do extra overtime in the summer months in return for the company sanctioning a 5-day week and staff summer holidays, it is unclear why the Union were now arguing that position. Country bus driving jobs were being advertised at this time at a rate of £24/10/- per week (minimum).

In the last two alone, the green country buses and Green Line services combined had made losses of two million pounds. For the first time in 23 years, on Christmas Day 1969, no buses or coaches operated from Amersham garage. The Transport (London) Act 1969 separated the green buses from the red; the red stayed with LT but the green were hived off for private enterprise to sort out; if they could. There were enormous problems based around a share capital of just £2! At the end of working on 31st December 1969 the Amersham Garage, staff and vehicles passed from London Transport to the newly formed National Bus Company subsidiary, London Country Bus Services Ltd.

Chapter 7   It's all Change on the Buses (1970-1985)

On 1st January 1970 control of London Transport was handed over to the Greater London Council who had no interest in managing the country area buses and Green Line coaches. In turn responsibility was transferred to the National Bus Company (NBC) who formed London Country Bus Services Ltd. (LCBS) on the same date. All staffs working for the country area were transferred to LCBS. The immediate difference seen by at Amersham was the new name transfers applied to the lower side panels of each vehicle. Posters were put up at both the garage and bus shelters announcing the takeover, other than that, initially there was little the public would have noticed. By March a new company motif was released to the press.

It is described in a black and white press release as being a green ring around London in which London Country will operate, the angled bars were claimed to give perspective and a hint of transport amidst green fields. We will see later the motif changed slightly when it was placed on the vehicles and became a golden yellow outline of the one shown here. Staff went on to name it "The flying Polo mint".

The above photograph was taken almost in front of the old A&D Amersham headquarters building on 11th April 1970. It shows 20-year old RT3612 registration no. MLL922 running on Route 353 out to Berkhamsted Station. The bus promotes "Green Rover" tickets priced at seven shillings a day. By August the price had gone to eight shillings, let's hope the adverts were changed in time.
Photograph courtesy of A B Cross.

The country area bus fleet would now stand on its own. The London Transport major bus overhaul works at Aldenham was still available to be used but that came with a hefty price tag. It was soon decided that maintenance would become a country garage's responsibility. In addition, up to now all posting of timetables and publicity had been done by LT's Central Headquarters' staff, now London Country Bus Services (LCBS) had to sort all these things out for themselves. Amersham garage was a well-run operation and its primary task at this time was to complete the full changeover to one-man operation (OMO). Drivers not already trained and operating as such were offered a £5.00 per week rise to take on the role. Conductors were offered training as drivers and they actually found the transfer to being OMOs far easier than did the conventional drivers. Those not wishing to become drivers were offered redundancy, some conductors refused and sat playing cards in the canteen until the Company came up with offers of other employment, or they found jobs themselves. Overall Britain was rapidly moving to a position where less staff would be required in many sectors; petrol stations moved to "self-service", J Sainsbury's old stores transformed into major supermarkets and "cash point" machines, having been launched in 1967 by "On the Buses" star Reg Varney, started to be seen on our high streets.

Across the entire LCBS fleet, 563 new OMO vehicles were acquired between 1970-3, however, the venerable old RT, RLH and RF fleet were kept running more easily than their replacements! Amersham bus electrician, Bert Chennery, remembered staff at Aldenham contacting the garage to remind them they still had an RT "float" body at the works and would they collect it? Needless to say, Aldenham were told they could keep it. Old maintenance routines had been shelved and unsurprisingly reliability dipped, this alienated both passengers and staff. The exodus of fare paying passengers continued unabated. The excellent RFs, already 17 years old, would soldier on for a while longer. A lovely photograph of one operating on Route 336 appeared in the Bucks Examiner in March 1970. The kindly RF driver had stopped to allow a row of ducks to cross the road by Skottowes Pond, Chesham. The double-deck RTs continued to be phased out despite their on-going reliability. On 27th June 1970 the Sunday Route 362 RT double-deckers were replaced by single-deck RF and MB-type buses. All this was in preparation for total one-man services.

Golden Rovers Launched

On 16th August 1970 Golden Rover tickets were launched. A 15/- (75p) adult ticket would give an unlimited days travel on both London Country buses and Green Line coaches (initially Route 727 was excluded). Child fares were 11/- (55p), ordinary Rover tickets were by now priced at 8/- adults and 6/- children. (By 1977 the Golden Rovers were £1.20 adult and 60p for under 14s).

Decimal Currency Day was 15th February 1971, the day everything changed.

Ron Bovingdon, driver, remembers that in the weeks before D-Day the Company sent round a double-deck "Instruction bus". Staff were shown a film on the top deck, it was all about decimal currency. John Hutchinson a newly qualified driver started very shortly after the big day and says *"It was also the final transition of total one-man operated buses for Amersham and we were all told that we were the first major operator garage in the country to move to "driver only" services. We had lost our final 8 conductors; the last Amersham based RT (driven by Mark Adlington) would run on the 353, for the time being double-deckers ceased to operate from Amersham. But even this monumental change was eclipsed somewhat by the entire Country's change over to decimal currency. Gone were our familiar LSD (Pounds, shillings and pence) with 12 pennies to the shilling and 20 shillings in the pound, instead we had just 100 new pence in the pound. We were all instructed that we could still take "old" money but had to give change in "new" money. Well, that was difficult enough in theory, but in practice for a bus driver trying to take dozens of very low denomination fares and having limited "new" change in his float, it was an impossibility. I used to run out of "new" money in no time at all and had to revert to giving change from the "old" money coming in. Passengers wanted to get rid of their pre-decimal money and would quite often give 2 x 3d and 6 x 1d for a 5 new pence fare! Boy was it stressful and it didn't settle down for ages. I always felt sorrier for the old folks who certainly thought you were diddling them by giving them far less "new pence" back in change than they expected."* (The final crew day out of Amersham was 19th February 1971).

The now obsolete half-cab style of double-deck buses with the driver sitting out front on his own was gone forever from the Amersham garage. However, for another four years a few conductor/driver operated vehicles would ply their trade in Amersham and Chesham as they still operated on routes like the 353 when starting from Windsor. 1971 was also the year that Wilf Brackley retired. Wilf had completed forty years' service starting out with the old Amersham & District Bus Co. Like Jim Chapman, he had seen changes almost beyond comprehension; he could transport your mind down the avenues of time with his recollections. He had seen many new vehicles arrive, serve their days and depart. It was now his time to step down and enjoy his retirement just as the thoroughly modern AEC SM-type Swift single-deck buses in green and yellow livery were introduced on all Amersham's 353 and 362/A services. The new Swifts were extremely good-looking buses with a double door arrangement. They were a shortened version of the Merlin (MB-type), being 33 feet 5 inches long against the Merlin's 36 feet 8 inches. A batch of nine SMs was delivered to Amersham in February 1971 (SM449-457). These were later supplemented by a few others providing additional service from the garage. However, the model generally gained a reputation for unreliability, it had poor heating and the coin change issuing systems regularly failed. There were also complaints of an underpowered engine. The SMs only lasted 8 years and were scrapped or sold off in 1979. As already said though, the Company's investment in maintenance had fallen way below the former standards of London Transport and it is always easy to blame the product.

From 1972 the corporate image of the National Bus Company had become mandatory, and to many observers the presentation sank to an all-time low. Experiments were made with a "pea" green RF but they finally settled on a sludgy green (known in the trade as Leaf Green) with white relief. These new paints dulled rapidly in the harsh bus wash and rapidly looked somewhat forlorn. Luckily for Amersham based vehicles, Brian Saunders painted them every 12 months before their yearly test. The once handsome green LT staff uniform was also replaced by drab grey. Finances were being rationalised, Councils were to start subsidising some loss-making routes but they would understandably try and seek to minimise any support funding. The numbers of buses running would inevitably fall drastically.

In the past there had been trouble on Route 353 when running late out from Gerrards Cross and back towards the garage. On picking up customers turning out from the cinema, periodically there would be young lads wanting to show off. It was not unknown for the boys to pile on and go upstairs, then proceed to remove light bulbs and throw them down on the conductor as they came up to collect fares. They then stampeded off the bus at Chalfont St. Giles laughing as they had secured a free passage. Things didn't necessarily improve with the introduction of single-deck pay as you enter vehicles. Some years later Brian Valder recalled:-

"A well lubricated lad boarded my SM vehicle at the Gerrards Cross cinema and asked for Chalfont St. Giles. When I got to The Pheasant, I shouted to the lad, who replied that he wanted to go down to the village. I told him this was the nearest this bus got to the village and suggested he got off otherwise he would be in Amersham next. The lad slopped off, but then picked up a stone and smashed the rear window of the bus. I stopped the vehicle and another passenger said "I'll get him for you driver", he gave chase and floored the lad with one punch. The police were called and the officer on duty gave the stone throwing lad a telling off and told him to go home, he felt he had been punished and suitably humiliated".

This photograph outside the Amersham Garage dates from this time. Brand new SM479 on the left alongside RF173 that harks back to 1952. Interestingly the nearly 20-year old RF has been chosen to operate the GREEN LINE coach route 710 (albeit only a shuttle to Uxbridge by this time), whilst the new SM is given bus duties on the 362. This RF had been given a makeover with interior strip lighting, twin headlights and curved windscreen. There surely doesn't look a two-decade age difference; such was the design quality of the RF. Green Line operations from Amersham ceased for a period after October 1972.
Photograph John Hutchinson collection.

Since the outbreak of war, now over 30 years distant, staffing Amersham garage had never been easy. In April 1972 one significant change took place, a woman was engaged and trained to drive buses. Carol Pesdee had been a conductress facing redundancy but she decided to stay with the company, for a while she helped her mother (Doris) who ran the staff canteen; finally, she was offered a place at driver school. Carol passed her test on 12th April and became Amersham's first female to be employed behind the steering wheel. It is remarkable to think that back in the early 1940s women had been flying all types of RAF planes, often single handed, but for years London Transport had resisted engaging them for bus driving roles.

As already mentioned RFs were renowned for their reliability but with their only dashboard instrument a speedometer, it meant that if they started to overheat there was no early warning.

There are plenty of stories relating to this very issue here are three:- Brian Valder, whilst driving an RF on a nice summer's day had the vehicle blow a sump full of very hot black oil over a pristine white Triumph Herald convertible, the hood was down! Luckily only splatters hit the car driver but the white paintwork was destroyed. The Company had to pay for a full re-spray and set of clothes for the unfortunate car owner. Maurice Gettings had his RF engine suddenly stop, there was momentary silence before a loud explosion and oil gushing out from a blown off filler cap. The dipstick had launched into orbit like a November 5th rocket. Engineers came out, repaired a water hose, refilled the vehicle with oil and water and it started like a baby, suffering no ill effects. Ron Bovingdon accidentally filled his RF's radiator from the bus wash watering can, by the time he got to Cholesbury the vehicle looked like it was floating in a bubble bath!

On 16th September 1972 this photograph of John Hutchinson driving RF305 was taken at Buckland Common with the vehicle operating on Route 348B to St. Leonards. It shows the transitional London Country branding, the old London Transport emblem on the front seems to have been thickly painted over but the Company's new motif yet to be applied. Ghastly tape has been adhered top and bottom of the destination blind window, allowing far more, newly abbreviated routes, to be accommodated on a single blind roll. The resultant visual area was a mere 8 inches high and difficult to read. The lovely old sign-post adds to the picture but the RF is looking a little sad as it nears the end of useful life.
Photograph taken by J G S Smith, courtesy of The Omnibus Society.

Former London Transport Country Area RLH44 had run on Route 336 out of Amersham Garage between March 1956 and July 1964. It was retired from passenger carrying duties in August 1970 and immediately converted to the form shown above. It was now used as a mobile uniform store and given the service vehicle bonnet no. 581J. It is understood that towards the end of its employed life it deteriorated so badly that it was towed from location to location to dispense uniforms and was withdrawn totally from service in April 1982. It is now in preservation as shown above.
Photograph John Hutchinson collection.

A locally distributed advert dating from April 1974 promoting One-Man Buses even though they had been running as such out of Amersham since February 1971.

By now the old, ever reliable, ex-LT vehicles were few and far between. John Hutchinson recalls *"I remember one Saturday we only had three SMs fit for service. We managed to borrow some more 20-year old RFs from other garages to cover our shortfall. During the course of that day the remaining three SMs had engine failure. On the Monday morning all Amersham's services were back to running early 1950s, ever reliable, RFs"* (story believed to be from April 1974).

When the notion of motor buses plying the roads of Amersham and Chesham was first muted back in 1919, a somewhat disgruntled resident wrote to The Bucks Examiner on 14th March that year and said *"I hope also for sake of the beauty of the country, and the artistic sense of those who have to see them, that the buses will be single-decked, and not plastered with music-hall and quack medicine advertisements."* Fifty-five years on from that published letter, London Country allowed buses to be literally covered in advertisements. Like them or loath them they became a regular vision on our beloved Chiltern roads and over the coming pages a few of them will be featured. It must not be forgotten that it did provide a useful revenue stream, which helped keep services running. However, some people complained they didn't recognise the buses and missed them!

August 1974 SM476 registration no. DPD476J "The Buckinghamshire Advertiser" liveried bus which was named "Bertha" by staff at the Advertiser. Amazingly all the advertising on this bus was hand-painted, vinyl transfer wrapping had not come on stream yet. Seen here parked up at Amersham Garage but ready to go out on Route 364 to High Wycombe. Photograph taken by Ian Pringle

New Bristol BL-type single-deckers were introduced on 5th January 1974 but could only display 3-digit route numbers, Routes 348A and 348B were jointly renumbered 349 and the 305A journeys became just 305. These BLs were to replace old RFs on the more sparsely trafficked routes. Their introduction caused a major problem at the garage, they were manual gearbox buses and half of MAs drivers only held licences for pre-select, semi-auto and auto gearbox vehicles. All had to be retrained and take another test!

This photograph dates from c1976. Bristol LH model, BL23 joined the Amersham fleet new in January 1974 but left after 5 years' service in this area. The new style "London Country" name was painted high on the roof to enable better selling potential from the side panel advertising space.
Photograph taken by G A Rixon.

A fabulous period shot of BL20 operating out on the Buckinghamshire country lanes in the mid-1970s. In this and the previous photograph it would be all too easy to crop out the vehicles that both buses are passing but I feel they add far more to the historic scenes.
Photograph from the Ron Bovingdon collection, photographer not recorded on the reverse.

By 1976 the decline in Green Line services across the network had reached a crisis point, either the name Green Line would be scrapped or it had to change dramatically. It was decided that a revamp should be tried and new luxury coaches were purchased the following year. New marketing campaigns were designed and the public started to warm to the new quality vehicles which were financed on a rental basis and would have a regular 5-6 year replacement cycle. Gone were the days of 20 years' service from venerable old coaches. The new vehicles were very modern looking AEC Reliance coaches, with bodies by either Duple (RB-type) or Plaxton (RS-type). Profits started to be made and Green Line moved towards the 1980s in much better shape. Overall the Company had lost £3.5 million in 1976 but reduced that to £2.6 million twelve months later.

Amersham garage had started 1976 with seven RFs still in its fleet but these would not remain for longer than a few months.

May 4th 1977 AEC Swift SM125 stopping at the garage to pick up on Route 353 before going on to Chesham and Berkhamsted.
Photograph John Hutchinson collection.

On 30th September 1977 High Wycombe bus garage was closed due to further LCBS cost cutting, all services were transferred to Amersham. The bulk of High Wycombe staff took redundancy but a few drivers did transfer. Frank Brown, a conductor with 3 years' service, was offered £145 redundancy but decided to move to Amersham and train as a driver. The number of vehicles at Amersham now grew by another 20 to around 55, not enough space was available and an agreement with the Council allowed for an area of the public car park behind the garage to be marked off for buses. The newly popular Green Line services also added a route from Amersham via High Wycombe to London Victoria numbered the 790.

A misty old morning in Gerrards Cross on 14th October 1977. SMA19 (JPF119K) running on route 790 into London Victoria. Amersham garage was allocated two new RB coaches for this route along with this SMA, the only one of its type to run from MA. It was rarely used on this route as it was considered under-powered.
Photograph from the John Hutchinson collection.

This 1978 rear view photograph of 41-seat AEC Swift SM510 DPD510J coming to journeys end for Route 362 as it passes along Botley Road towards Ley Hill Common. SM510 was new in June 1971 and worked out of Amersham from March 1976 until it was sold exactly three years later.
Photograph N Lamond collection.

As mentioned earlier, the SMs gained a reputation for unreliability such that there were times when staff were left idle with no serviceable vehicles to operate. Replacement for the SM-type vehicles started towards the end of 1977 when eight Leyland Nationals were brought in. The entire replacement programme took two years to complete. Narrower Bristol BN-type single-deck buses also started to make an appearance operating from Amersham. They were 7' 6" wide compared to the BL's 8' 0" width.

In 1978 the "London Country *Matters*" staff magazine did a feature article all about the Amersham garage and its employees. Chief Depot Inspector Gerry Coe recalled that when he had joined in 1938 there were nearly 100 vehicles stationed there. He well remembered the old Qs, Cubs and STs, he felt the peak was soon after the war when 150 drivers and 100 conductors were employed. Former Hemel Hempstead driver cum inspector Reg Murray, who had only just transferred to become Chief Inspector at Amersham, commented "It's an easy garage to settle down in. They are a good crowd with a happy atmosphere". Reg's sentiments will account for the reason so many staff dedicated a lifetime's work to the Amersham bus garage.

Chapter 8   The Chiltern Link (1980–1985)

More changes came when, on 13th April 1980, local services began to be branded "**Chiltern Link.**" This not only involved vehicles from Amersham Garage but High Wycombe as well.

Following a recent overhaul, this 1972 built Leyland Atlantean AN13 MPJ213L is seen here turning at the War Memorial Chesham. This 1980 photograph shows the new "Chiltern Link" emblem.
Photograph John Hutchinson collection.

Chiltern Link's green buses from Amersham now ran to new destinations such as Marlow and Desborough Castle (a large council estate adjacent to a public house of that name in High Wycombe). In the last chapter we saw that after the closure of High Wycombe garage in 1977 there were approximately 55 vehicles at Amersham. By 1980 this had fallen back to just 41 and would reduce further this year to 37, ten of which being Leyland Atlantean (AN-types); double-deckers having returned to the garage for the first time in nearly a decade. Once again, the delights of upper deck travel could be experienced locally.

Author's thoughts on riding on the top deck.

The upstairs front seats provide something of a motion picture "in camera" view of all that surrounds you ("in camera" means held in a private room, camera meaning "room" in Latin). Those viewing are largely unseen by those upon which you spy. You note everything that happens from a safe and single vantage point. A seat costing no more than any for your fellow passengers yet has the status of the front seats in the "Grand Circle" at a theatre. A person waiting at the upcoming bus stop puts their hand out or the bell rings, you plan to stop as well as the driver. The waiting young mother starts to fold the child's push-chair; the pensioner gets their bus pass ready. All is prepared for the leviathan to stop and for the hiss of brakes and door mechanisms. You look at everything except the upper-deck passengers from the vehicle passing in the opposite direction; the drivers acknowledge each other with that very British lift of one finger, you sit quietly observing all below. Studying the car drivers and their passengers who reside at the foot of your personal moving cliff face. Peering into gardens, hidden to those unable to stand fifteen feet in the air. Your mind is free to roam as far as your bus carries you.

This Amersham based 1980 Duple Dominant Express coach on AEC Reliance chassis was nearly new when this photograph was taken at High Wycombe. Registered EPM129V, given fleet no. RB129. The roundel at the back is the celebratory symbol for Green Line's 50th anniversary (1930-1980). The highlight of this year was a rally from Golders Green to Crawley in which approximately 130 vehicles spanning the years from 1930 made the run.
Photograph John Hutchinson collection.

This Duple bodied AEC Reliance coach EPM135V became part of a small fleet business set up by Fred Ivins son of Charles Ivins. Charles was the chairman of the original Amersham & District Motor Bus Co. founded in 1919. Fred, and later his son Stewart, used the name "Pride of Bucks" in honour of the 1919 business. Ex Green Line RB135 (RB standing for Reliance Blackpool) also took part in the rally to Crawley. This vehicle was not based at the Amersham garage.
Photograph 1 taken at Wembley coach park. Both photos from John Hutchinson collection.

This Leyland National SNC159 started life as a Green Line coach but is seen here behind Amersham Garage having been downgraded to bus duties. It had been stripped of its Green Line livery but the painter (Brian Saunders) had deliberately not repainted the window frames, hence this rather nice but incorrect London Country colour scheme. Sadly, it didn't last long before Head Office ordered it to be given their standard finish. These designated SNC Leyland National coaches were fitted with luggage racks and comfier high-backed vinyl seating.
Photograph taken by Vic Zealey from John Hutchinson collection.

A London Country "Chiltern Link" Bristol LH bus on Route 336 waits at Ley Hill in the early 1980's. These buses had been around for 10 years at this stage although their reliability was considered poor, drivers also didn't appreciate their bouncy ride, heavy steering and stiff clutch pedals. Registration TPJ 59S has fleet no. BN59.
Photograph N Lamond.

Back in Chapter 5 we saw how London Transport had used pre-war double-deck buses, with their roofs cut off, as so called "tree loppers". In 1963 LT purchased five Ford Thames Trader vehicles with bodies specifically designed by their "Road Services Department" to replace these old vehicles. A design feature of the bodywork allowed part of the upper sides to be lowered to create an open and unguarded working platform. Subsequently London Country inherited some of these vehicles and as we enter the 1980s two senior Amersham drivers volunteered to take on their operation in the North West Area, enter Norman Freeman and Bob Keen. Maurice Gettings would later go on to replace Bob. This would become a part-time function they performed whilst still remaining available for bus driving rotas.

Norman Freeman and Maurice Gettings were originally allocated this Thames Trader lorry as they embarked on a seemingly hilarious part-time career; tree lopping for London Country. The lorry dated back to 1963, registration number 965ELR, LT had given it the service vehicle fleet number 1241F.
Photograph from Norman Freeman.

Norman says he was given two days training and a selection of hand tools along with the lorry! As a team they set about the work and stayed in post for the next 9 years, it seems they enjoyed a laugh a minute companionship. Their story has many hilarious encounters over the years but one stuck in their minds. Bring on the day of the big storm in October 1987, Maurice had cut all the low branches from a very big tree and was sitting in the cab of the lorry. Norman was cutting the higher branches from the top of the lorry when suddenly, the tree was no longer there; it was completely blown down, luckily away from the lorry. If it had fallen towards them, surely both Norman and Maurice would have been seriously injured, if not killed in the crushed lorry. When Norman went back to the cab, Maurice had no idea what had happened and asked Norman what the strange noise was? Norman, still shaking, announced "let's get out of here" and they went to the nearest garage, High Wycombe, for a strong sweet cup of tea.

From 20th July 1980 a joint venture with National Bus Company's (NBC) Oxford South Midland operation saw new, Amersham based, Green Line coaches running a 290/790 fast service between Oxford and London Victoria. The 790 additionally serviced Heathrow. Fortunately, this kick started a brief new heyday period for the name "Green Line," just as it had reached its 50th anniversary celebrations. However, most passenger traffic was into Victoria at the start of the day, not returning until the end, therefore some coach drivers found themselves with long idle spells parked out at the Battersea coach park. This was not making efficient use of staff and "Green Line Days Out" to visitor attractions up to 25 miles away e.g. Hever Castle, Sheffield Park Gardens, The Bluebell Railway, Woburn Abbey and Windsor Safari Parks were offered to the public. However, they were not a huge success and did not last.

Also, at this time we see the management at Amersham garage taking further steps towards women's equality, with their first appointment of a female D/I (Depot Inspector). An article in "London Country Matters" Autumn 1980 was titled "Woman's touch", it reported that Hilary Dellar had been appointed to the role. Hilary had joined the workforce as a driver one year earlier, so this was highly commendable rapid promotion. The outgoing D/I (Mr G Willmont) had clocked up 31 years' service, fairly big shoes to step into for Hilary. Mr Willmont had been presented with a tankard and a step ladder; apparently, he had never managed to get into his loft and was planning to investigate it in his retirement!

The role of training new drivers was ongoing and this Amersham coded Bristol BL6 was spotted in York Road, Kings Cross in January 1981. The yellow banded livery denotes a training vehicle.
Image courtesy of Barry Wilkinson.

The first ever open day to promote the Amersham Garage took place on 25th July 1981. For those in the community that took a time travelling "Tardis" trip down to old Amersham on that sunny summer day a spectacle awaited that brought a smile to the faces of hundreds. Here are some photographs from a wonderful day staged in the town.

1981 - The garage has its first OPEN DAY

A replica vehicle depicting the early days of the "General", bearing the bonnet number B340 it provided delightful rides for a lucky few and a chance to experience what a trip on the N6 (later to become the 336) might have felt like in the 1920s.
Photograph N Lamond.

1981 Open Day - continued

AEC ST922 is still a familiar sight at the London Bus Museum, Brooklands, although it has now been restored to its original "Tilling" livery.
Photograph N Lamond.

GS15 was new to London Transport in October 1953, the nearest it got to working at Amersham was a spell out of Garston before being sold off in March 1969. My wife and eldest daughter pose for the camera.
Photograph N Lamond.

RT3491 and STL2692 shown in post war livery inside the garage. RT3491 was always a red central area vehicle, it was new in March 1952 and received its country green livery sometime after being sold off in August 1973. STL2692 always wore the country green, it was a post-war vehicle being delivered in February 1946 and worked some time at Watford and Garston before being withdrawn in May 1955.
Photograph N Lamond.

Another photograph from this 1981 historic event features preserved London Transport 1939 34-seat coach TF77 (FJJ774) parked alongside the garage's own Bristol BN58. I have not seen any photographic record that TFs operated out of Amersham in their active days but one recognised enthusiast's website does say that TFs 14 and 15 were at Amersham in 1953 immediately prior to withdrawal. So, you never know the wheels of this rare type of AEC single-decker may have stood on the very spot nearly 30 years earlier.
Photograph N Lamond.

1981 Open Day – continued

The final photograph from this 1981 event puts faces to a couple of the names given mention in this book. L-R Arthur Whitting, Brian Valder, Ron Bovingdon. Brian and Ron went on to become Inspectors and Arthur moved across to driving Underground trains. All have their National Bus Company jackets on for the special day.
Photograph from Ron Bovingdon's collection.

AMERSHAM'S WINTER WONDERLAND JANUARY 1982

Two lovely photographs from January 1982, when the snow came. Top: RB25 has been trapped half in and half out of the garage and judging by the dirt has been doing a few journeys in these conditions. Bottom: A row of SNBs parked in the Dovecot Meadow car park behind the garage.
Images courtesy of Barry Wilkinson.

This stunning looking 1979 AEC Reliance coach is operating out of Amersham Garage on GREEN LINE Route 290 (Oxford – London). YPL99T bonnet no. RB99. It was at MA between July 1980 and withdrawal from Company service at the end of 1983.
Photograph John Hutchinson collection and not credited on the back but I have seen this photograph credited to Geoff Rixon elsewhere.

Announcements were made in March 1982 of numerous service cuts to reduce the Company's running costs. Most of Amersham Garage's routes were affected one way or another. The 309, 336, 349, 335, 353 and 359 all suffered reductions in operation which were blamed on low usage by passengers. The only bonus was the introduction of a 336 express service between Little Chalfont and Watford; this was distinguished by a blue destination blind and would start at Ley Hill. The following January, in a bid to win more new passengers for its Green Line services, off-peak (after 9:00am) fares were cut to attract train and car users. The "February Fares Fighters" offer meant the maximum single fare would be £1.00. This resulted in journeys of more than 12 miles being cut in price by 50%. There were a few exclusions; 290, 291 and 790 north of High Wycombe along with airport services. Bernard Davis, Green Line's Commercial Manager said "our fares are now well below current train rates and we believe that people who give us a try will come back again". To enhance the Green Line push, in May 1983 new turbo-charged Leyland Tiger coaches with luxurious interiors were introduced. These coaches bodied by Duple (TD) or Plaxton (TP) replaced the AEC Reliance (RBs).

This photograph of TD13 was taken in January 1984 to the side of Amersham Garage.
Image courtesy of Barry Wilkinson.

On Saturday 13th October 1984 this 53-seat Green Line TD14 working out of Amersham Garage was photographed at Oxford Bus Station working the 15:00 departure on Route 790 to Heathrow. This Leyland Tiger coach with Duple Dominant bodywork was new in April 1983 and was withdrawn in October 1988.
Photograph John Hutchinson collection.

In September 1983 YPD114Y (shown above) featured in a press release that followed a competition to create a TV jingle. Frank and Jeane Viney from Amersham won themselves a colour television set, courtesy of London Country Green Line. Entrants had to complete the sentence "I like travelling by coach because…." The Viney's winning slogan was "I like travelling by coach because it is cheaper by far than putting petrol in the car". Green Line assistant manager Norrie Thomas presented the Vineys with their television set in front of the coach.

A rare photograph from July 1984 of TP9 on the short lived Green Line, Aylesbury to London, Route 788. "Charlie" Singh is the driver. "Charlie" had joined LT in the mid-1960s and transferred from High Wycombe garage when it closed in 1977. Sadly, he has now passed away, Frank Brown remembers him as "a laid-back fellow, always willing to help a colleague."
Photograph taken by John Golding.

Marylebone Station to close!

For some time, rumours had circulated that British Rail were planning to close Marylebone Station. The National Bus Company were so excited about the prospect that they spent a lot of time and money planning to take it over to become a Green Line hub. In fact, in early 1984 their ten-million-pound outline plans were revealed. The idea was to use up to ten miles of track bed from Northolt or Neasden as a super express coach highway direct into Marylebone. An expensive project that would certainly have cut journey times and taken a predicted 250,000 annual coach journeys away from London's crowded roads. Chiltern Railways went on to have the last laugh about the idea and now regularly tops train service reliability league tables.

Ron Bovingdon recalls a very serious accident happening around this time. Two Amersham based Leyland Nationals were travelling in opposite directions on Route 353. They were on the London Road between the Garage and Chalfont St. Giles when they were involved in a head-on collision. Drivers John Murdock and Mark Witchell were both trapped in their cabs, several young passengers were also hurt. Another bus arrived on the scene, a Leyland Atlantean, and that driver used a hack-saw to cut through one steering wheel to give relief to one on the trapped drivers. It was later claimed that the accident had been caused by a learner driver pulling out from a side road. Mark Witchell was off work for a long while recovering.

Parking additional vehicles behind the Amersham garage attracted the attention of vandals, especially those intent on siphoning fuel. Sadly, some vehicles were damaged around this time. In early 1985 a Leyland National SNB515 (registration EPD515V) was very badly damaged in an arson incident. Luckily a lady walking her dog in the fields behind rushed to alert unaware garage staff who put the blaze out with extinguishers. Her quick action surely saved a total loss of the bus as it was repaired by Amersham staff and placed back into service some months later.
Photograph courtesy of Ron Bovingdon.

Amersham Garage celebrates its 50th anniversary with an open day, 19th May 1985

John Hutchinson, on the left, is shaking hands with TV celebrity Roy Castle. John's idea for this open day raised nearly £1000 for Heritage House Special Needs School in Chesham. To mark the occasion, John is wearing an original 1950s LT driver's uniform. Mark White, Steve Roberts and Dave Bassett, make up the other three figures, each were founder members of the Amersham & District Motorbus Society.
Photograph taken by Anthony Bassett.

The official programme for this event also provides the following additional information:-
The garage currently employs 104 Drivers, 6 Depot Inspectors, 5 Road Inspectors, 31 Engineers headed by Superintendent Cliff Street and a Garage Foreman. It houses 44 buses and 14 coaches (10 Leyland Atlanteans, 29 Leyland Nationals and 5 Bristol LHs; the coaches are all Leyland Tigers, 9 with Plaxton Paramount bodies and 5 with Duple bodies).

This photograph was taken on Wednesday 14th August 1985 (the actual 50th birthday). To mark the day, two preserved vehicles (RLH48 and GS1) embarked on a local "parade" run. Afterwards group of enthusiastic garage employees gather in front of RLH48 (a former member of the MA fleet when in her green liveried days), the nose of GS 1 can just be seen. L-R Tony McEwen; Stuart Milton; John Hutchinson; Eddie Friar; Ken Redrup; Chris Tilbury (Engineer with head in engine); Reg Murray, Garage Traffic Superintendent; John Townsend, Engineer.
Photograph from the John Hutchinson collection.

August 24th 1985 "Birds Garage Ltd" liveried Amersham based Leyland National SNB344 is photographed at High Wycombe. Note the older style of telephone exchange number for Slough/Gerrards Cross area omitting the "1" after the zero. The first of this new batch of advertising liveries was shown to the local press in February 1984 (two vehicles for Chiltern Estates); the days of the old green local bus was coming to an end. At the time of this photograph, Amersham garage was home to 58 London Country buses and Green Line coaches.
Photograph John Hutchinson collection.

A 290 (Oxford – London) operating out of Amersham Garage, this time a 1983 53-seat Leyland Tiger with Plaxton Paramount bodywork (hence TP). TP21, registration A121EPA, viewed in a rather empty Victoria Coach Station. It was moved out of service from Amersham in October 1986.
Photograph John Hutchinson collection.

A longer version of the TP designated coaches was appropriately given the fleet lettering prefix of TPL. Here is a recollection from John Hutchinson about one such vehicle.

Green Line runs over some coppers!

"*I was driving one of the longer versions of the Leyland Tiger; it was not in service at this time. Boy was it a hot day and so I decided to open the passenger door to let some extra fresh air in. I was just coming off the Marylebone flyover when the internal cab door accidentally flew open, freeing my cash box to take to the air and fly. Like some misshapen piece of space debris, it disappeared through the passenger entrance. It became more misshapen when it hit the road and ever more so when my rear wheels ran over it, spreading coins on the tarmac like some pirate treasure. I had no alternative but to stop, take my life into my hands and started to pick up the coins. Luckily a number of amused drivers stopped, coming to my rescue and I was able to retrieve the loot and get back on my way. I think I took a few bent coppers back to Amersham with me that night*". John also says "*Operating some of Amersham's Green Line rota in the 1980s could be real fun, we built up a very nice relationship with the commuters and on Fridays many regulars boarded the coach with wine and finger food. They didn't forget their drivers who were often handed a pork pie and soft drink when stationary in the heavy traffic. By the time we got to Stokenchurch, the young secretaries on board were sometimes a bit giggly! I remember another time, having done all my London stops I diverted to some side roads to avoid huge tailbacks on the A40, unluckily a very badly parked car stopped my progress. A number of male passengers recognised the problem, got off the coach, bounced the car out of the way and we made it through. Those were the days*".

Chipsteak, peas and chips £1.32 declares a sign up on the right of this mid 1980s view of the staff canteen counter. L-R: Driver Rex Puddifoot; Sandie Lally (later to become Drabwell), Canteen Manageress; Tracey, Canteen Assistant.
Photograph taken by John Hutchinson.

A photograph also thought to be from the mid-1980s has engineering staff members Mick Freeman and Mick Davidson standing either side of Mary Wells who had been a conductress for a number of years in London Transport days. Mary had taken early retirement on 23rd March 1971 at the time when all vehicles moved to one-man operation. The RF will be a preserved vehicle on a visit to the garage.
Photograph courtesy of Amersham Museum.

One final photograph featuring a "Chiltern Link" branded Bristol BN57. This time showing a rear view and featuring the often-seen advert at that period – "DAN DAN THE DATSUN MAN".
Photograph from the Ron Bovingdon collection, no credit on the reverse of this original photograph taken in Chesham in the early 1980s.

Mud, mud glorious mud – recalls Kevin Hull, Bus Fitter 1984-1990.

I had just come on shift, it was about 3:30pm, I was out on the forecourt moving a bus and realised water was flowing around my feet, lots of it. It was tainted brown and getting worse. A mud landslide was starting to engulf the Amersham garage. After a series of utility-based road works on Gore Hill, a water main burst (a 36 inch one we were later told). A million gallons of mud thick water poured down the hill and into the garage. Within 30 minutes staff were trapped in the canteen; inspection pits and toilets were filled, the water flowed right through us and down to the river. With all electrics gone we couldn't even re-fuel the returning vehicles. I spent that night ferrying buses to the Alder Valley depot at Newlands to use their diesel pumps. With true determination, a grand clear-up was embarked upon by staff and only the bus wash remained out of action for any length of time.
Nothing quite like it for cooling the blood!

Chapter 9   De-Regulation and Closure of MA (1986-1992)

De-regulation of local bus services came in during 1986 and London Country was broken up. This was done as part of a Government privatisation plan to create a more competitive market and counter non-profitable routes being subsidised by busier ones. In the process a number of loss-making services were handed to the local authorities for tendering. These became dark days for the industry and passengers, some smaller bus operators would pick and choose when they operated a route, especially if they had another job on the day that paid better! In October Amersham garage passed to London Country North West (LCNW). This was a newly formed company that covered garages at Amersham as well as Garston, Slough and Hemel Hempstead. The group operated some 300 buses from these sites. Buckinghamshire County Council insisted on retendering routes and this saw many services being transferred to smaller operations with lower overheads. The "Chiltern Link" brand disappeared from sight.

Amersham LCNW driver Eddie Friar leads the way in support of Paraplegic Athletes.

Far sighted bus driver Eddie Friar became an unexpected star when he managed to obtain and donate one hundred and twenty-two trophies to support the 1986 Junior National Paraplegic Games held at Stoke Mandeville. Sports and Social Clubs from thirteen country bus garages also sponsored this event. They can all rightly pat themselves on the back for being very early adopters of what has become a world-wide phenomenon following the London Paralympics twenty-six years later.

It is believed Leyland National SNB307 was only at Amersham between October 1987 and June 1989, it displays early LCNW livery featuring a light green waistband and "North West" triangle just visible after the fleet name. Here it is over the pit for some remedial work. Kevin Hull an Amersham bus fitter (1984-90) said the record time Mick Freeman, he and two other chaps had changed an engine in a Leyland National was 7 hours, "Amersham garage got on with work, other garages took days to do the same job".
Photograph John Hutchinson collection.

A lovely sunny day for AN195 to be making its way through Amersham on Route 353 bound for Slough. This photograph shows the first London Country North West livery although it does seem that MA garage painter Brian Saunders didn't have a ladder long enough to touch up the top front corners of this Leyland Atlantean.
Photograph taken by John Golding.

This is a photograph taken midway through a day when the extra, peak time, Green Line coaches have returned. It also shows we are in the transition period when the coach livery was changing, the new colour scheme on show to the right.
Photograph taken by John Golding.

SNB311 was at Amersham for a similar time period as SNB307 shown previously, but has been re-branded for NORTH WEST LONDON COUNTRY.
Photograph John Hutchinson collection.

This photograph taken in January 1988 shows Leyland Tiger NTL5 operating out of Amersham in the new Green Line livery. NTL designation being taken from the previous owner National Travel London. The destination blind beneath the windscreen says "NATIONAL HOLIDAYS". These were tour buses that "National" used for holidays all around the country. The rest of the destination blind would have had lots of different resorts and major towns on it. In total three of this type were stationed at Amersham for a period. If used on regular Green Line routes then the driver had to stick a number on the windscreen, if he forgot then the passengers christened them "the mystery bus". These 40-foot long vehicles had notoriously heavy steering.
Image courtesy of Barry Wilkinson.

The most famous of all RTs, number 1, spent some time being stored at Amersham in the 1980s. It was often just tucked away down the right hand side but is on show here probably at the time of the first ever vintage running day organised by John Hutchinson.
Photograph courtesy of Amersham Museum.

Driver Billy Gahan always smiled, captured here alongside AN242 around 1988. Oops what has happened to the Leyland's front spot lights, surely not another cost saving exercise? Notice the AN behind Billy has a black front panel painted with "Welcome on board".
Photograph taken by John Golding, John and Billy were best friends.

This scene at the foot of Gore Hill shows the old Fox's Outdoor Clothing shop and also a yellow liveried British Telecom lorry. AN195 running on Route 362 has unusually not gone straight on, passing the garage and up Whieldon Street, it may have been that The Broadway was closed for the annual fair.
Photograph taken by John Golding.

A nice inside shot of the garage and the rear of AN168 in LC North West livery.
Photograph taken by John Golding.

"Bus Company in Shock Buy-Out"

This was the Bucks Examiner front page headline for 15th January 1988. The story went on to say that "The Amersham bus garage together with its parent company London Country Bus (North West) has been bought out by its own management". The new owners had purchased the concern from the National Bus Company and they pledged a more attractive and efficient service for Chiltern users. This latest private industry takeover following the de-regulation of bus services was announced by Dennis Ord, LCB Managing Director and one of those involved in the buy-out. Mr Ord promised a number of things, firstly mini-buses would be introduced on local routes, providing high frequency personalised services. Company livery would change to provide a smarter cleaner look and staff would be given new uniforms. Mr Ord also said new staff pay structures had been agreed.

On 11th May 1988 a bus giving disabled passengers greater access went on display at the Amersham garage. London Country (North West) failed to take on any of these vehicles. Later in the year a charity started running "Dial-A-Ride" services in Amersham and Chesham which did provide special disabled access.

Near disaster happened in the summer of 1988 when repair men working on the Amersham garage roof accidentally set fire to it. Within moments, flames were leaping ten feet in the air and the emergency services called. Staff rushed to move vehicles to the outside and the fire brigade soon extinguished the blaze. Fortunately, no persons nor vehicles were damaged.

Despite the new Amersham by-pass being built, buses pulling out from the garage actually seemed to find things worse. Traffic was running faster through the Old Town and parking abuses increased. At times buses were forced to double-park when stopping for passengers. A letter on the matter, from K G Andrews, London Country (North West) was published in the local press in October.

All was not well under the new management, in the eyes of many of the staff "if this was Maggie's vision of privatisation then she could stuff it". Parts were in constant short supply such that even bus light bulbs were being swapped around vehicles. One day John Hutchinson remembers engineer Bill Grafton, who had been at the garage since the 1930s, saying *"I have never seen our fuel tanks so low, they are lower now than they ever got during the war"*.

A new dark green and silver stripe livery made its entrance on the vehicles and the drivers were given the promised new uniforms; green blazers and ties. Both certainly did enhance the overall image. The area also finally said goodbye to its Bristol buses that had seen service for the last 14 years, passengers often said they gave a "bumpy ride" so they may not have been missed too much. By February 1989 certain bus services were being cut back due to lack of use. A few weekly journeys on the 353 to Ley Hill and some on the 362 and 345 were axed. The following month, the Amersham garage's fate was effectively sealed; it was announced in the local press that the Council had reluctantly passed Tesco's plans to develop the adjacent former Brazils factory and slaughter house into a supermarket and car park.

In August 1989 the Lee & District Bus Company was acquired by London Country North West. A decision was taken to start a local high frequency mini-bus operation called "**The Chesham Connection",** with routes radiating out from the town. Within a few weeks a number of second-hand MBD mini-buses were transferred in and based at the former Lee & District garage on Chesham's Waterside. This meant that the longer distance services coming into Chesham could terminate there. See Appendix 1 page 44 for full details of each route operated.

Saturday 30th September 1989 and "Chesham Connection" service can be seen operating a Dodge mini-bus MBD21 registration no. D862NVS as a "FREE BUS" taking passengers up to Great Hivings (fares were normally charged). Note the old Eastern Electricity showroom behind, now a more familiar sight to us as Café Nero.
Photograph taken by Vic Zealey founder member of A&D Motorbus Society, courtesy of The Transport Library (Robin Fell).

These services proved uneconomical to run and the scheme failed after about a year, a shame as I remember this service driving up Kiln Lane, Ley Hill and into Letchfield to take elderly Mrs Parker right to her door. Now that is personal service not matched in the previous 70 years.

With the takeover of Lee & District, LCNW acquired an additional seven coaches that continued to operate the old company's school and private hire business. Their liveries were not changed although they were moved to be based at Amersham garage. The only interaction they performed with the scheduled daily services were an odd occasion when a coach on Green Line (GL) duties might break down and no spare GL coach was available, then a Lee & District liveried coach might have been sent out. Transporting some very happy passengers, as the Lee and District coaches had much more luxurious seating, music and a free coffee machine!

Time lapse photography nearly 60 years apart ....

An amazing pair of photographs. The first one taken outside Coleshill Church when a young Wilf Brackley driving an Amersham & District bus encountered a wheelbarrow abandoned in the road. Wilf hadn't been with A&D long at the time, having started in February 1931. The second from 1989, set up to recreate the event in order to promote a charity fund raising vintage bus running day (70 years since the founding of A&D Motor Bus Co.). Wilf retired from driving buses after 40 years but at 86 clearly still had a good straight back for lifting the barrow. The day raised money to send special needs children from "The Saturday Club" on a dream holiday to America.
Photograph 1 courtesy of John Hutchinson who also arranged the charity raising vintage bus running day. Photograph 2 courtesy of The Bucks Free Press.

The end is nigh for Amersham Garage

Less than two years after the management buy-out led by Dennis Ord, in September 1989 an announcement by London Country North West was made that Amersham garage was being sold. The 140 staff, who naturally felt extremely let down, later discovered the site was also to become part of the new Tesco's, in fact their filling station area. The Bucks Free Press ran a large article about the closure and a photograph accompanied the piece showing a dozen or so very unhappy workers. Engineer Mick Davidson told the newspaper that the staff had been promised by management they would all be kept together in new premises, that promise was now being broken. It seemed that engineers and cleaners were facing imminent redundancy. Over the weekend of 2nd and 3rd December 1989 the majority of Amersham's buses and bus services were relocated to the former British Road Services (BRS) depot in West Wycombe Road, High Wycombe.

The now virtually empty Amersham garage retained about six SNBs, had Route 294 running from there and housed Chesham's mini-buses. Also remaining at Amersham, for a short time before they were sold, were the Lee & District coaches. The overall reliability of the mini-buses made the Chesham Connect service uneconomical and it closed on 15th September 1990. Chesham bus services now reverted back to as they had been prior to their introduction in October 1989.

Servicing facilities at High Wycombe were so poor that the now doomed Amersham garage was pressed back into service as a back-up maintenance unit for a period of time. All the while awaiting its fate from the wrecking ball.

Leyland Atlantean AN168 at the foot of Gore Hill in 1990 or 91. Displaying London Country North West branding and operating on Route 353. This 1978 built vehicle is recorded as being written off in an accident in January 1992. It is an extremely rare sight to see it operating on the, by now single-deck, 353 route. With Berkhamsted Station as the terminus, this vehicle could not pass under the bridge adjacent to the station; it would therefore have to do a tricky reverse turn in front of that bridge.

A manoeuvre that was fine in crew days when the conductor could look out for danger but they were now long gone.
Photograph John Hutchinson collection, John is the driver of this 353.

On 12th October 1990 London Country North West was in turn acquired by Luton & District Transport. Operations at High Wycombe's West Wycombe Road were transferred to the town's Cressex Industrial Estate.

Leyland National SNB430 YPL430T new to London Country in December 1978 and withdrawn in August 1995. Seen in this photograph branded as "CHILTERN BUS" following the takeover by Luton & District in late 1990. L & D also adopted a red and cream variant of the livery on some Leyland Nationals that may have strayed into our area, despite operating from Aylesbury and Luton.

Photograph John Hutchinson collection.

133

Norman Freeman said his sad farewells and retired on Saturday 28th March 1992 having started at the garage in 1954.

The Amersham Garage finally closed its doors on Thursday 2nd April 1992. But unlike the event in 1954 when they had been closed as a mark of respect for the funeral of Maureen Percival, this time the event went off without ceremony. It is seen here, fenced off, awaiting demolition, which didn't happen for many months. The white painted garage to the left of the photograph is one of the remaining old A&D buildings that went on to survive until 2017. The Luton & District "Hoppanstoppa" bus looking more like an ice-cream van was on loan as a crew rest room to enable staff operating on Route 353 to have a place to sit in and eat their lunch. (Apologies for the somewhat obvious join of two old non-digital photographs).
Photograph John Hutchinson collection.

The wrecking ball finally gets to work...............................

The demolition of the garage took two weeks longer than planned as the contractors engaged on the job said it had been built so well it would "have lasted 200 years".
Photographs from the John Hutchinson collection.

For some months after the closure of the garage the Company opened a small administration office in the parade of shops just before the Memorial Gardens in Old Amersham. About six buses operating on routes 336, 353 and 362 were still out-stationed in the car park behind the old garage. Ironically these were the three routes that were the mainstay of the original operation built up by Amersham & District Motor Bus Co. from their foundation in 1919.

The service continues, a lovely shot of TPL93 on Green Line route 290 at High Wycombe in July 1992.
Photograph John Hutchinson collection.

This final photograph from 1993 shows how a handful of vehicles were subsequently parked in Dovecot Meadow car. It also illustrates that the era of green country buses blending harmoniously with our countryside and dating back to A&D days of 1919 was well and truly over.
Photograph John Hutchinson collection.

The staff at the Amersham garage always felt a great affinity with their customers; the local press and staff magazine alike often reported on the good deeds done by drivers and conductors over the years and the gratitude felt towards them. A few have already been mentioned in these pages but I don't want to close without recognising some more. In 1984, driver Hugh Jackson encountered a person having an epileptic fit whilst travelling on his bus. Hugh's first thought was to seek help as quickly as possible, so rather than waiting for an ambulance he drove off route to get the person to The Chalfont Centre for Epilepsy, the patient receiving attention in double quick time. A rather sadder case occurred when a bus crew encountered an attempted suicide by the cutting of wrists. Fortunately, they were first-aid trained and managed to stem the blood flow in time for an ambulance to get that person to hospital. The string of almost weekly accounts of lost children, escaped livestock and the more general saving of pets could fill a book on its own. The camaraderie of staff and the work of the garage's Sports and Social Club was also a great force for good, both in raising money for local worthwhile causes and for the well-being of staff. Having been started by the old Amersham & District Bus Company nearly 60 years earlier it remained a great joy to many who worked for the Company and remained active throughout the 1980s. People like Wally Lally excelled both at billiards and snooker along with successes for Mick Freeman and (father) Norman Freeman in golf competitions. Over the years the Club took children on trips to places like Chessington Zoo and Thorpe Park, they arranged open days for the public and enthusiasts. Their teams at darts, bowls, pool and fishing all did well and after 25 years of absence a football team was re-launched and we mustn't forget some cricket success by the LCNW team. Even some of the children on the Chessington trip won the London Country children's painting competition later that year. And finally, a mention for John Hutchinson, who has helped me so much with this book; he won a class shield when he entered 3-year old coach (TP13) into the Bristol Festival of Transport. For a number of years in the later 1980s John ran busman's holiday trips to south coast resorts like Eastbourne, inviting former London Transport and London Country staff. So much is lost if a place of work shuts down and only memories like these are left. Where will those good deeds come from when driverless vehicles arrive on our streets? No cheery driver to ease an old person's loneliness as another part of our heritage will fade into distant obscurity.

Chapter 10   Looking back over the years

In our journey over the 60 years from 1933 to 1992 we have seen huge changes in the fortunes of the staff entrusted to operate our local bus services. Before the war, the male only job of a driver or conductor carried some prestige. The dark days of war, where everyone on the home front worked to breaking point, showed what an essential role the humble bus played in our endeavour towards victory. Women joined that role and toiled as hard as any man. In the two decades that followed, there was unease and resentment among the staff, they felt let down even betrayed, as their roles became taken for granted. The public grew ever more independent from the bus. But the crews never let themselves down; far from it, as we move into the 1980s the staff at Amersham garage rally to raising money for charity and finally starting the Amersham & District Motor Bus Society. A club which, through running their old vintage buses on summer weekends, brings joy to grandparents, parents and children alike.

In May 1924 Sir Stanley Baldwin (three times Prime Minister in the inter-war period), in part of a very nostalgic speech to The Royal Society of St George, had said "The sounds of England: the tinkle of the hammer on the anvil in the country smithy, the corncrake on a dewy morning, the sound of the scythe against the whetstone, and the sight of a plough team coming over the brow of a hill". These reminiscences were as precious to him as ours are to us today and over the course of this book and its forerunner volume "The Pride of Bucks" I have dipped into a nostalgia that afflicts generation after generation. When the original A&D story began in 1919, letters to press amounted to concern on the damage that motor buses will cause to the environment as well as the mental wellbeing of the townsfolk. Many mourned the loss of horse drawn power and riled against "the stinkin moty-car". Recently I was talking to a lady who lived in Latimer during the war and she fondly recalled Dell's private buses that served her tiny village in those austere days. With a wry smile she said we called the bus "IFIT", that was if it turned up. But in the end, we came to rely upon and love our local buses.

During the A&D period of operation, countless technological advancement was made that altered the countryside dramatically. Some were adopted with barely a murmur, others, like telephone boxes caused some concern. In 1933 A&D were no more, having been taken over by London Transport. From certain quarters there was a sadness that the old A&D had become a local institution that would be sorely missed. Over the ensuing years we witness the demise of our almost traffic free roads, the loss of our wonderful Chiltern wild flower meadows and our dark green liveried buses that so blended in with the countryside. However, refuges like Old Amersham still look wonderfully weathered and valorous, having witnessed all. Roads have widened and been dressed with a confusion of signs, lining and lettering as the authorities seek to control our ever-sprawling population.

I saw a sign outside an antique centre at Boxmoor this week, it said "Let the past be your present". I hope these pages have been the mantle for creating heart-warming memories, stirring the juices of your mind. Whether you gain nostalgia from the whole book or just the era from which you have greatest recollection, I do hope you have enjoyed a trip down your own memory lane. Transported in mind down these avenues of old time. Ron Bovingdon, who started as a young, long haired, conductor in the 1960s and rose to Senior Duty Manager, said in 2018, with a deep thoughtful look on his face, "Good times, we were like a family".

It seems that every generation prefers things to remain untouched, however, I notice my grand-children are passionately excited about steam locomotives and definitely love the A&D vintage bus running day. Most though, are now times lost in far-away mists.

I am going to catch the 362A back to my village.

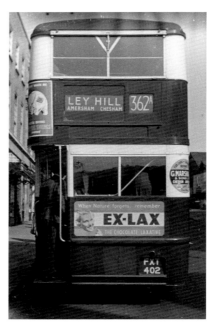

STL2679 taken in October 1949, I was born the previous month.
Image courtesy A B Cross.

WRITTEN BY NEIL LAMOND, LEY HILL, 2018.
THE END

Appendix I — Routes operated from Amersham Garage

(unless otherwise stated)

This appendix is made up from as much information as could be gathered from maps (after 1948), timetables (mainly before 1948), local press notices and PSV scheduling notes. It only covers the period from the re-numbering of old A&D routes during 1934 until garage closure in 1992; it does not mean that a route stopped in 1992. Some route numbers were used in adjacent areas (not covered by Amersham garage) at times either prior to or after the dates shown. The information below cannot be considered totally accurate but is designed to provide the reader with a reasonable account of the routes that were operated. On longer routes buses and coaches would have been operated from garages at each end of the route. From December 1989 as a prelude to the eventual closure of the garage at Amersham, longer routes and Green Line services were operated from High Wycombe.

COUNTRY BUS ROUTES

Route 305, 305A

Route 305 was A&D's Routes 6/10 on their 1933 timetable.
The 305 ran throughout the period of this book 1934 to 1992. It was a popular service from Uxbridge to High Wycombe via Gerrards Cross, Chalfonts, Beaconsfield, Loudwater.
Most 305 journeys were between Gerrards Cross and High Wycombe until November 1968. 20th Feb. 1971 Route 305 experimented with Jordans Village – Beaconsfield Tue and Fri. From Oct 1977 – Apr 1980 a Penn – Beaconsfield service also ran as the 305.
Jordans ceased to be served by any service after Apr 1998.
Route 305A was a weekday only service that operated between Uxbridge and Chalfont Common with some journeys being extended on to Horn Hill until November 1968. After that date the routes were converted to one-man operation, and Horn Hill was no longer served. It ran between 26th March 1947 and 1973.

Route 307

Known to have operated between 1941 and 1944, running a service from Chesham via Hemel Hempstead to Harpenden. Operated from Hemel Hempstead LT garage.

Route 309

From 1977 listed as running from Amersham to Rickmansworth via Chorleywood. It was running before this date from Chorleywood to Harefield via Rickmansworth. In 1982 it was re-numbered 337 after a suggestion made by John Hutchinson.

Route 316, 316A

Route 316 was A&D's Route 16 on their 1933 timetable.
Chesham to Hemel Hempstead via Bovingdon. The 316 was withdrawn for a period during the war but re-instated on 5th April 1944 with STs operating it. Otherwise the 316 ran from 1934 to 1965. From 13th May 1936 it was run by Hemel Hempstead LT garage and later at times by the local independent Rover Bus Co. who fully took over running of its weekday schedule from 6th

May 1964. For the next 17 months Amersham Garage supplied RFs to run a Sunday shuttle service between Amersham and Ley Hill via Chesham, this was finally withdrawn on 3rd October 1965.
An additional service, the 316A ran from Chesham to Whelpley Hill, this service did not run for the full duration on the 316 route.

Route 332

Amersham – Stanley Hill – Quill Hall Estate
Appears on maps from 1960 to 1977 but is recorded as starting on 16th October 1956 when it started running school services from Amersham garage to Quill Hall Estate.

Route 335, 335A

Watford – Windsor via Rickmansworth, Chorleywood, Chenies, Chalfont St Giles, Gerrards Cross, Slough.
335 appears on maps and timetables from 1934 to 1977
335A was operated by Amersham Garage from September 1942 to October 1945 between Chalfont & Latimer Station and Newlands Park for staff of North Mercantile and British Insurance which was located there during the war.

Route 336, 336A, 336B

Chesham to Watford via Amersham, Chenies, Chorleywood, Rickmansworth. Until 1933 this was National's N6 route. Until May 1936 it had run on to Berkhamsted after Chesham. Until December 1942 the route was shared with Watford Garage vehicles after that date exclusively Amersham vehicles used. Lowbridge ST-types 1933 to June 1950 then RLH-types until October 1965 when RF-types took over on 336 passing through Amersham.
336 appears on maps and timetables from 1934 to 1992.
336A Rickmansworth – Loudwater Estate
336A appears on maps from 1952 to 1971
336B operated on Sundays between Little Missenden and Northwood Station via Amersham, Chenies, Rickmansworth and Mount Vernon Hospital. It partially replaced Green Line Route 703.
336B appears on maps from 1964 to 1968.

Route 337

Ley Hill to Rickmansworth via Chesham, Amersham, Little Chalfont, Chorleywood, Heronsgate.
337 started in April 1982 and appears on maps from 1984 to 1986.

Route 345

Amersham (Old Town) to High Wycombe via Gt. Missenden, Prestwood, Hazelmere.
345 appears on maps from 1985 to 1986

Route 348, 348A, 348B

Route 348 was A&D's Route 8 on their 1933 timetable.

Chesham Moor to Buckland Common, after 26th March 1947 extended to St Leonards via Chesham, Bellingdon, the first ever motor bus service to St. Leonards.
(1965 map) Buckland Common or St Leonards, Bellingdon, Chesham, Cholesbury, Wigginton, Tring.
348 appears on maps and timetables from 1934 to 1977 but was known to have been withdrawn for a period from 1st July 1942 when its service was covered by 394A.
The 348 was withdrawn between Chesham Moor and Chesham Broadway in July 1942, but continued to operate between Chesham and Buckland Common. It was re-instated after a while and from 1st November 1944 started at Chesham Moor rather than Chesham. 1972 Route 348 withdrawn Chesham Bdy – St Leonards but extended from Hyde End via Sth Heath, Lee Cmn, The Lee, Swan Btm and Chartridge.
348A Chesham to Pond Park Estate (1965 map Pond Park, Chesham, Cholesbury, Wigginton, Tring.). 348A appears on maps from 1956 to 1973 but started at least as early as 7th October 1953.
348B 1968 – 1971 Hyde End or Chesham Moor to Chesham via Chartridge; 1972 348B withdrawn Chesham Bdwy. – Chartridge but extended from Chesham – St Leonards.
Gt. Missenden – Wendover now not serviced.
348B appears on maps from 1968 to 1972

Route 349

The route took over services from the 348A/B in January 1974, the change was made because the new narrower bus blinds could not cope with A and B suffixes.
1974 map Chesham Moor to either Pond Park or St Leonards via Chesham town. 1977 map shows taking in Bellingdon and Chartridge but not St Leonards. 1985 map shows it going out to Wigginton from Belllingdon and St Leonards with a loop out to Hyde End and into Amersham.
349 appears on maps from 1974 to 1986

Route 353, 353A

Route 353 was A&D's Route 3 on their 1933 timetable.
Berkhamsted to Windsor via Chesham, Amersham, Chalfonts, Gerrards Cross, Slough.
Initially this route ran to Ley Hill after its Chesham stop but from 13th May 1936 it was diverted to Berkhamsted after stopping at Chesham. However, by the 1980s it was running back to Ley Hill at times.
During the summer of 1964 a 353 Express was introduced on Sundays. This was a limited stop service to speed up the journey. Most journeys operated between Chesham (Nashleigh Arms) and Windsor, a journey of 52 minutes and over 30 minutes faster than the conventional 353. The previous Sunday hourly service on 353 was reduced from hourly to 2 hourly and the express version operated two hourly. It was not repeated the following Summer and the 353 remained two hourly.
353 appears on maps and timetables from 1934 to 1992
353A Chalfont Common to Windsor via Gerrards Cross. 7th Jul 1973 353A Chalfont Cmn – GX extended to Windsor instead of 305A.
353A appears on maps from 1973 to 1974

Route 359, 359A

Route 359 was A&D's Route 9 on their 1933 timetable. It is shown on maps and timetables from 1934 to 1992 although ceasing to be operated from Amersham for varying periods.
Amersham to Aylesbury via Gt. Missenden, Wendover. From 1940-42 it was just running Chesham to Hyde Heath. To cover for the wartime withdrawal of Green Line coaches from Wednesday 30th September 1942 it started running from Amersham to Aylesbury via Chesham jointly operated with Eastern National Omnibus Co. until 1952 and thereafter with United Counties when they took over the Midland operations of EN. UC stopped their operation in May 1964. 20th Feb 1971 359 now to serve Sth. Heath, Ballinger and Lee Cmn. In April 1982 started just running to Chesham on Mon, Wed, Fri & Sat and Amersham Tue & Thur.
359A was shown as an Amersham to Hyde Heath service in 1940 -42.

Route 362, 362A, 362B, 362C

Route 362 was A&D's Routes 1/2 on their 1933 timetable. It was still running in 1992.
Ley Hill to High Wycombe via Chesham, Amersham, Holmer Green, Hazelmere. In 1980 the route gained an extension from High Wycombe to Marlow for a period.
362A 1934 – 22nd June 1974 Ley Hill to High Wycombe via Chesham, Amersham, Holmer Green, Widmer End; except during 1940-3 when it only ran from Ley Hill to Chesham
362B 1937-56 Penn to High Wycombe, Sunday service.
362C 1936-40 Ley Hill to High Wycombe via Amersham. Service started in May 1936.

Route 364

Chesham (Pond Park Estate) or Ley Hill to High Wycombe via Amersham and Widmer End. Service started in the area on 22nd June 1974 to replace 362A but by 1977 Ley Hill was not shown as a final destination on maps. Service is still shown on 1980 map but not on a 1983 map.

Route 369, 369A

Route 369 was A&D's Route 19 on their 1933 timetable it operated until July 1935.
1934 only Aylesbury to Windsor via Gt. Missenden, Slough.

Route 369A was A&D's Route 5 on their 1933 timetable.
1934 only Gt. Missenden to Chesham via Amersham.

Route 372

18th September 1972- 1977 Amersham to High Wycombe via Stanley Hill, Hazelmere. Service started to serve Brudenells School.

Route 373

Route 373 was A&D's Route 13 on their 1933 timetable. 1934-77 (but not during WW2 also not shown on maps 1962-70) service ran from Beaconsfield to High Wycombe via Penn. In 1951 running Leyland Cubs. In 1961 was running GS buses out of MA usually designated for 332.

Route 387

Route 387 1985-86 ran in a large loop from Amersham (on the hill) to Beaconsfield, Penn, Hazelmere, Hughendon Valley, High Wycombe, Marlow, Hambledon, Fingest, Lane End.

Route 393

1939-40 Amersham to Gt. Missenden. Service started 25th Sept. 1939, ceased in December 1940. Operated with Leyland Cubs.

Route 394, 394A, 394B, 394C, 394D

Route 394 was A&D's Route 4 on their 1933 timetable.
Hyde End to Gt. Missenden via Chesham, Chartridge, Lee Common, Ballinger, South Heath. 20th Feb 1971 394 withdrawn between Gt. Missenden and Chartridge.
394A Chesham Moor to Great Missenden
394A appeared on maps from 1948 to 1968
394B Chesham – Chartridge - Ballinger
394B only appeared on maps in 1957, but was certainly running in 1949.
394C Hyde Heath – Amersham
394C appeared on maps from 1943 to 1957
394D Chesham – Swan Bottom and Kings Ash
394D service ran from 1956 to 1958 (replacing a service previously provided by Lee & District).

Route 396 (A photograph exists showing 23 in use shortly after LPTB takeover).

Route 396 was A&D's Route 23 on their 1933 timetable.
1934 only Chesham to Beaconsfield via Winchmore Hill, Penn.

Route 397

Route 397 was A&D's Route 7 on their 1933 timetable.
Chesham Moor to Tring via Chesham, Hawridge, Cholesbury, Wigginton.

Route 398, 398A

Route 398 was A&D's Route 20 on their 1933 timetable.
1934-40 Chesham to Beaconsfield via Stanley Hill (Amersham) and Coleshill (Magpies).
1941-1992 Amersham (Quill Hall Estate) to Beaconsfield via Coleshill.
398A 1937-69 Amersham to Winchmore Hill via Coleshill. From 16th October 1956 provided Quill Hall Estate with a service.

Route 455

This was a High Wycombe to Uxbridge route run mainly from High Wycombe garage. It appears on maps and timetables from 1934 to 1977. Circa 1936 photo of T-type vehicle on route operating out of Amersham. 1960's PSV reports state Amersham RT vehicles from 305 route used on 455.

CHESHAM CONNECTION – MINIBUS SERVICES – LONDON COUNTRY NORTH WEST
Services started in 1989 (did not run on Sundays) and ceased 15th Sept 1990.

Minibus A
Chesham Broadway – Little Hivings – Chesham Broadway

Minibus B
Chesham Broadway – Beechcroft Road – Chesham Broadway

Minibus C
Chesham Broadway – Hilltop Estate – Chesham Broadway

Minibus D (Started 4th December 1989)
Chesham Broadway – Hilltop – Botley – Ley Hill – Chesham Broadway

Minibus E (Started 4th December 1989)
Chesham Broadway – Berkeley Ave - Chartridge – Chesham Broadway

Minibus F/G (Started 4th December 1989)
Chesham Broadway – Chesham Moor – Chesham Broadway

Minibus A1 (Started 28th April 1990)
Chesham Bdwy via Berkhamsted Rd – Addison Rd – Lyndhurst Rd – Upper Belmont Rd

Minibus A2 (Started 28th April 1990)
Chesham Bdwy via Bellingdon Rd – Hivings Hill – Upper Belmont Rd – Greenway – Lynton Rd – Addison Rd – Berkhamsted Rd.

Minibus A3 (Started 28th April 1990)
Via reverse of Minibus A2 route.

GREEN LINE ROUTES

Route B
Chesham – Wrotham via Amersham, Rickmansworth, Harrow, Marble Arch, Victoria, Elephant & Castle, Foots Cray, Swanley. **OR** Aylesbury – Wrotham via Wendover, Amersham, Rickmansworth, Harrow, Marble Arch, Victoria, Elephant & Castle, Foots Cray, Swanley.
First appeared on official L.T. maps in 1934 and last appeared in 1939. Service ceased on 1st Sept. 1939. In August 1940 route 35 started as a replacement. AEC Regal T Class vehicles used throughout.

Route R
Chesham – London (Oxford Circus) via Amersham, Gerrards x.
This express coach route was started by the old A&D company in 1931 and finally numbered as 17 in their very last timetable dated November 1933. The number 17 would not have appeared on the coaches. As Route R it first appeared on official L.T. maps in 1934 and ceased after 1939. It started as a route from Chesham but after a few months of running from there its licence was invalidated and it had to start from Amersham. On 8th Jan. 1936 it was re-instated

to run from Chesham. Service ceased on 1st Sept. 1939 but was re-instated 7th Jan. 1940 then in August 1940 this route became route 34. AEC Regal T Class vehicles used throughout.

Route L1

Chesham – Great Bookham via Uxbridge, London. Weekend service recorded on official L.T. coach map 1936. The L1 service was a weekend extension to Chesham of the weekly L service. It is unlikely this weekend service was run from Amersham. It ran from 30th May to 10th October that year.

Route 33 (Formerly Route Q)

1941 Limited wartime service only High Wycombe - London. All Green Line services finally withdrawn on 29th Sept. 1942.

Route 34 (Formerly Route R)

4th Dec 1940-42 Chesham-Amersham-London (Oxford Circus)
Limited wartime service only. All Green Line services finally withdrawn on 29th Sept. 1942.

Route 35

4th Dec 1940-42 Aylesbury-Amersham-London (Victoria)
Limited wartime service only. All Green Line services finally withdrawn on 29th Sept. 1942.

Route 290

1980-92 London-Oxford via Shepherds Bush, Uxbridge, High Wycombe, Stokenchurch. Started 20th July 1980. From 1982 Route 290 also called at Beaconsfield.

Route 291

2nd July 1980-86 London-Thame via High Wycombe, Stokenchurch. In January 1982 extended to cover Haddenham.

Route 292

1982 Amersham-London via Holmer Green, Hazelmere, High Wycombe.

Route 703

Amersham-Wrotham via Rickmansworth, Harrow, Victoria, Sidcup.
Started 3rd April 1946, withdrawn 3rd November 1964.

Route 704
Wycombe – Slough – Heathrow, started July 1991

Route 705

Wycombe – Uxbridge, hourly route started July 1991

Route 709
Chesham – Godstone via Amersham, Gerrards X, Oxford Circus, Croydon.
First appeared on official LT maps in 1948 (started 12th Nov 1947) withdrawn 31st Oct 1965.

Route 710

Amersham – Crawley via Gerrards X, Oxford Circus, Croydon.
From 11th Nov 1968 became OMO and covered Amersham to Baker St. until 22nd Feb 1971 when it just ran to Uxbridge. First appeared on official LT maps in 1948 (started 12 Nov 1947) and withdrawn 13 Oct 1972. It was temporarily withdrawn 3-20 Oct 1954 due to staff shortage at Amersham Garage.

Route 724

3rd April 1946 – 12th November 1947 High Wycombe – London (Oxford Circus).
1966-72 (not run out of Amersham) High Wycombe-Romford via Amersham, Watford, St Albans, Welwyn Garden City, Harlow (One man operated). From 1973 ran from Staines to Romford.

Route 725

Chesham-London via Amersham, Gerrards Cross, Uxbridge, Shepherds Bush to Oxford Circus. Started 16th June 1946, withdrawn 29th October 1947.

Route 737

1989-90 Amersham/High Wycombe to Heathrow via Beaconsfield

Route 746

1984 only. The route operated between Slough and Milton Keynes. A short-lived route taking in Ashridge, Berkhamsted, Chesham, Beaconsfield and Farnham.

Route 788

1982 (January) - 1988 Aylesbury-London via Amersham, Denham
Frank Brown (driver) states it was withdrawn in Sept 1988, having been out-stationed at Aston Clinton since Oct 1986.

Route 789

1982 Chesham to London via Amersham and the Chalfonts. Only ran from 16th Jan 1982 to 2nd Oct 1982.

Route 790

High Wycombe – London Victoria
Amersham started running this route on 1st October 1977. From July 1980 -1986 re-routed to take in Heathrow and away from Uxbridge Road.
As Route 290 1981 route.

Appendix 2   The advertisement splashed Leyland Nationals

This 1976 built Leyland National SNB200 LPB200P was liveried for "Chiltern Estates" and shown to the press (along with a sister vehicle) in February 1984 when the company was 5 years old. It remained like this until being restored to a green livery in September 1987 after which it did not return to Amersham. Seen here on Chesham's Broadway.
The photographer is not recorded but we are grateful for its historic record, from John Hutchinson's collection.

This 1977 built Leyland National SNB342 UPB342S is liveried for "Christopher Rowland" Estate Agents. It spent all its years from 1977 to 1992 working out of Amersham. It underwent this "colourbus" repaint in 1985.
The photographer is not recorded but we are grateful for its historic record, from John Hutchinson's collection.

This 1979 built Leyland National SNB465 BPL465T is liveried for "Holtspur Kitchens" Beaconsfield & Amersham. It stayed at Amersham until 1992. It was overhauled in September 1986 and possibly gained this livery at that time.
The photographer is not recorded but we are grateful for its historic record, from John Hutchinson's collection.

This 1979 built Leyland National SNB513 EPD513V was liveried for "Holtspur Kitchens" of Beaconsfield in October 1985 it stayed at Amersham until 1990.
The photographer is not recorded but we are grateful for its historic record, from John Hutchinson's collection.

This 1977 built Leyland National SNB342 UPB342S liveried for "Hampton Rowland" Estate Agents in August 1985, photographed at Luton. This bus was re-liveried twice more for the same company before being transferred from Amersham after closure in 1992.

The photographer is not recorded but we are grateful for its historic record, from John Hutchinson's collection.

This 1979 built Leyland National SNB 500 DPH500T was liveried for "Olympic Kitchens" of Chesham in June 1988. It remained at Amersham until closure in 1992 and continued to sport that company's advert.

Photograph taken by Daniel Hill.

Two very nice views of SNB461 BPL461T Liveried for "Practical Car & Van Rental" outside Amersham garage. This bus was built in 1979 and got this paint job late in life, it is believed to date from 1990. It stayed at Amersham until closure in 1992.

The photographer is not recorded but we are grateful for its historic record, from John Hutchinson's collection.

Taken around 1988 SNB471 BPL471T liveried for "Birds" car sales company. This 1979 bus had been advertising Super Tile of Gerrards Cross in 1984, it received this makeover in June 1986. It stayed at Amersham until closure in 1992.
The photographer is not recorded but we are grateful for its historic record, from John Hutchinson's collection.

This 1977 Leyland National SNB344 UPB344S is liveried for "Birds BMW" of Gerrards Cross. It seems to have only been at Amersham until 1985 so this photograph must have been taken before the end of that year.
The photographer is not recorded but we are grateful for its historic record, from John Hutchinson's collection.

Delivered new to Amersham in April 1979 Leyland National SNB454 YPL454T is seen here liveried for "Prophets BMW" dealer of Gerrards Cross. It is not recorded when this livery was applied but the vehicle did stay on at Amersham until closure in 1992.
The photographer is not recorded but we are grateful for its historic record, from John Hutchinson's collection.

"Super Tiles & Baths" SNB 471 photographed in August 1984 outside the garage.
Photograph taken by John Golding.